Also available at all good book stores

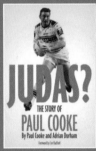

9781785312052

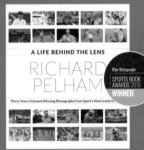

9781785315466

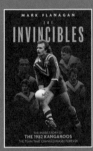

9781785315268

9781785314469

9781785314025

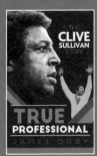

9781785313103

MATCH
OF MY LIFE

ST HELENS RLFC

MATCH
OF MY LIFE

DAVID KUZIO

First published by Pitch Publishing, 2021

Pitch Publishing
A2 Yeoman Gate
Yeoman Way
Worthing
Sussex
BN13 3QZ
www.pitchpublishing.co.uk
info@pitchpublishing.co.uk

ISBN 978 1 78531 547 3

Typesetting and origination by Pitch Publishing
Printed and bound in India by Replika Press Pvt. Ltd.

Contents

This book is dedicated to my wife Chris, sons Ryan Adam and Jack Freeman and my late daughter Kate – I love you all for supporting my dreams. It is also dedicated to those suffering with mental health issues, keep fighting and stay strong.

Author's Acknowledgements

First of all, I would like to thank Jane Camillin at Pitch Publishing for having the confidence once again to allow me to write a book in their Match of My Life series. In my honest opinion, I think every professional sports club, whether that be a rugby league, football or cricket club, should have a book like this. And I will do my best to ensure rugby league is well promoted by continuing to write these books.

Writing a book is difficult at the best of times; you cannot get through a project like this without the support of your family. For reasons you will discover later, it has been a difficult time for me so having my wife Chris, sons Ryan and Jack, mum and dad Kathleen and Adam, older sister Karen and mother-in-law Margaret all encouraging me to keep going has allowed me to finish this project.

I have to take time to thank every single player who contributed to this book, whether it was by myself phoning them, emailing them or interviewing them in person. You all made this book possible and it has been nothing short of an honour listening to your tales about St Helens. From interviewing Ray French at a Super League launch, speaking to Paul Wellens on the phone, organising a Face Time call with Dave Fairleigh or talking with Tommy Frodsham in his garden, it's been an honour to put your memories into print.

I'd also like to thank former St Helens physio Janette Smith for agreeing to write the foreword for this book. In this day and age, women play a prominent role in sport, and rightly so, but back in the eighties and nineties not many women were involved in rugby league. Janette was a familiar face on the touchline as she worked wonders with the injuries to the players, so I felt it was right for her to be involved.

I have already mentioned that you cannot write a book like this without the help of your family, but that is the case with your friends as well. Simon Atherton has been one of my best friends for years and he is very friendly with Phil Veivers, so over the years I have managed to build my own friendship with Phil and although he is a bad influence, he has some great stories to tell. Special mentions have to go to: lifelong Saints fan Rory Appleton, who constantly messaged me to see how I was and how the book was going as well as putting me in contact with Tea Ropati; long-standing Wigan fan Adam Conroy, who provided some information when I was struggling to find it; and Christy Abbott for the late-4night message asking if Tommy Frodsham would be good for the book. Also, thanks to Scott Whittle and James Wood, who combined to help get Paul Loughlin involved. Thank you for your help and interest, it means a lot. I actually didn't know it would be this much fun adding the names of Wigan fans into a book about St Helens – they will hate it, but I do appreciate their help.

Everyone who contributed to this book being published, I thank you all from the bottom of my heart. It means a lot. And to my youngest boy Jack, you haven't a clue that every time you came into my office and took everything off the shelves, I was working hard to get this finished. Just keep being yourself, little mate.

Dave Kuzio

4 July 2020

Introduction

I debated long and hard on whether or not to divulge the following information. I do not support St Helens. In fact, I am a Wigan fan.

There, I said it, and before you dump the book in the nearest bin, please hear me out. I am a Wigan fan and I have been since 1986 and I have watched them and reported on them all around the world. But I am a rugby league writer and I take my role very seriously.

I want to be one of the best writers out there and this is my fourth book. Two of my other books are on Wigan Warriors and Barnsley FC – my two teams. And being honest, writing about those teams is quite easy because I have been a part of their success over the years as a fan.

I felt if I really wanted to test myself, I needed to choose a topic I was not very fond of and would find it hard to get excited about. I chose to write this book on St Helens, and in all honestly, I have loved it. Hearing the stories of all the great players who have played for Saints over the years, was an absolute joy.

A lot of my friends have questioned why I would do this, but if I can take pride in a book like this and deliver the best I can, then I will be a happy man. This is not a stitch-up job; this is all genuine and it is probably my best book, to be honest, because of how difficult the subject matter is.

After I wrote the one on Wigan, I wanted to do the Saints one right away. I got in touch with someone at the club to see if they could help me get some players. At first, they were helpful, but I received an email saying he had heard I was a Wigan fan and wouldn't help me after that.

So, the book was put on the back burner, then after I finished my Barnsley FC one in 2018, I got to work on this one. Unfortunately, during 2019 I suffered quite a few mental health issues and my confidence completely disappeared. I was a shell of my former myself and I doubted whether I was a good writer. To be honest, I couldn't bring myself to do any work on the book. I had a load of interviews recorded, but I couldn't transcribe them. I was embarrassed and ashamed that I couldn't put my heart and soul into this project.

I'm glad to say that I am on the mend and I am taking it one day at a time. In June this year, I finally woke up and realised that this book needed to be finished and people actually wanted to read it. I have worked tirelessly ever since, and hopefully this book is something all Saints fans can be proud of.

Enough about that. How did this book finally come together? Whenever you work on a project like this, you always have a list of players you want. But unfortunately, there isn't a phonebook available that just has former St Helens players' names in. I started to use Twitter and LinkedIn to see which players would be interested.

Some reply and some don't. Sometimes it can be soul destroying when you know a player would be ideal, but they don't want to get in touch.

One player I knew I could count on was Phil Veivers. I have got to know Phil quite well over the years and he is someone I trust dearly. I was introduced to him by my friend Simon Atherton and we often meet up for a few drinks. They are nice evenings, until Phil decides to come back from the bar with a tray of Sambucas. Then he is evil.

So, Phil was a dead cert to be involved, but getting other players wouldn't be that easy. When I have written my other books, I've always gone home excited to tell the family who has agreed to take part. My whole family are Wigan fans and my eldest lad is a Barnsley fan like me, so in my other projects they have been excited to hear who I have got and what they have to say. It wasn't the case with this one and my wife threatened to make me sleep in the garage when I said, 'I've got Tommy Martyn for the book, should I do the interview here?' After a few choice words, she decided to post a picture on social media of our huge German Shepherd – Chewbacca – with the caption, 'Tommy, we are waiting for you'. It's safe to say, we did that interview over the phone.

In all seriousness, my family have backed this project no matter where their allegiance lies. I think they are just happy that I seem quite content and relaxed when writing about the game I love. I had better not print the response my wife made when I told her I had interviewed Louis McCarthy-Scarsbrook – because, as we know, 'rugby league is a family game'.

The first interview I did for this book was with Keith Mason. We had a long chat on the phone, and he spoke with great pride about playing in a Challenge Cup Final for Saints. He went on to talk about his new projects with his acting career and his new comic book. I thought, 'This stuff is gold, just what the book needs.' Then a few days later, I noticed he had done a number of interviews with other members of the rugby league press, so it would kind of be old news when the book was released. That didn't matter though, I knew I had a good interview to get this thing rolling.

I don't care who you are, if you have been following sport for a long time there will be players you have liked and admired that have never played for your club. I have taken a lot of stick over the years for this, but one of my all-time favourite players was Paul Newlove. I used to get comments like, 'How can you like him, he's a Saint.' And, 'You can't honestly like him.' Well the truth is, I liked Paul Newlove when he played at Featherstone Rovers and Bradford Northern, so I'm not going to suddenly not like a player because he has a red V on his jersey – that is not how it works. When I finally got an email and text from him saying he would love to be involved, I was over the moon. He was the final piece of the puzzle for me.

Now, I still had to get through this interview without sounding like a complete fan boy. Luckily for me, the interview was done over the phone and he couldn't see the stupid grin on my face, or that I had been pacing around the front bedroom of my parents' house waiting to phone him.

One of my favourite interviews in the whole book has to be with Dave Fairleigh. I'll admit one of the reasons I wanted Dave in the book is because the Best Man at my wedding, Paul Heaton (no, not that one), is a massive Saints fan and his favourite player is Dave Fairleigh, so I wanted to do the interview so he would go and buy a book.

I contacted North Queensland Cowboys to get in touch with Dave, as I thought he still worked there. The club got back in touch and said, 'Daisy doesn't work here anymore.' They gave me his mobile number and believed he would be OK with it. I was excited that I had his number, but I was now wondering whether or not to ask him why they call him 'Daisy'. It turns out the nickname is pronounced 'Daisy' but not spelled that way – he explains later on, trust me. Most of the interviews I conduct last between 10 and 15 minutes; you can get a lot of information in that time and seeing as I hate transcribing interviews, it's better for me. Well, this one didn't last 15 minutes; once I had finished my Face Time call with Dave, it had been 36 minutes. My first thought was 'that was amazing'. My second was, 'Oh no, I have to transcribe all that now.' It was worth it.

Through writing this book I have managed to strike up a friendship with a former player that I didn't actually have earmarked to be a part of it. A friend of mine – Christy Abbott – messaged me asking if Tommy Frodsham would be good for the book. I thought, 'yes, absolutely'. I remember Tommy playing for Saints in the eighties and this book is not meant to be about the superstars whose stories you have heard a thousand times. I spoke to Tommy a few times and he got something down for me to use, then I went to his house and we had a further chat. We also have plans to do another book down the line about St Helens – watch this space. He is a really great bloke.

As the book started to take shape, I realised I needed maybe a couple more chapters to be happy with the overall word count. I started to send out more messages and requests, but I was quickly running out of time. Then one morning I received a message that finally made my wife take notice of the book. Kevin Iro had messaged saying he would love to be involved. Now, with my wife being a mad Wigan fan, she was interested and it was an honour to interview the Beast.

I could go on all day about how each interview went, but I won't. This book is about the players and the pride they have for the shirt of St Helens. I hope you enjoy the stories and the selection of players I have chosen.

I have mentioned before, it's not easy to get everyone you want. There are some players not in the book who I tried to get, but I am more than happy with the ones involved. They have taken time out of their lives to reminisce about their time with the club and I can never thank them enough.

I hope you enjoy reading this book as much as I enjoyed conducting the interviews.

Dave Kuzio

7 July 2020

Foreword

By Janette Smith

First of all, I would like to thank David Kuzio for asking me to write the foreword for his book. I am truly honoured to do so.

My time at Saints ran from October 1989 until January 2001. Women physios were a rarity in rugby league at that time so when Alex Murphy and Eric Hughes asked me to join, the then chairman Eric Latham wasn't sure if a woman would 'work' and he wouldn't offer me a contract. Eleven years later, it seemed one wasn't necessary.' A male physio and my ex teacher at Wigan at the time said a woman physio will never be accepted in rugby league, why not do women's hockey?! The rest is history!

I was blessed to work with an amazing set of players over the years and several amazing coaches, both at Saints and on international duties. I was blessed to be the first woman to sit on the bench at Wembley and the first woman to go on tour with a Great Britain side in only my second season at Saints. I then went on to sit on that bench on numerous occasions thanks to the amazing skill and talent of our boys, and I managed to visit Australia five times and New Zealand twice.

When I first arrived at Saints, I remember Chris Arkwright telling me he was Harry Pinner for a whole season and seeing as I didn't know a lot about rugby league, I had no idea who he was. At that time, the players must have been having a right chuckle to themselves due to my naivety!

I was gutted when Alex Murphy got the sack, but I remember Eric Latham saying 'Don't worry love, coaches come and go but physios tend to stay.' He was correct. Then along came the amazing character and gentleman that was Mike McClennan, along with Tea Ropati, Jarrod McCracken, George Mann, Apollo Perelini, Vila Matautia, plus the great Shane Cooper who was already there. A fabulous Kiwi contingent of amazing, lovely lads and their families who will remain friends forever, as will all my players.

The idea was apparently that Shane gained experience from Mike and later took over the coaching role but sadly, as is usually the case with the politics of clubs, that never happened.

Our first Wembley was an awesome experience, we beat Widnes against all odds in the semi and were narrowly defeated at Wembley, which was devastating. It's no place for losers as Eric Hughes once said to me, but we went on to have many successes at Wembley after that – they were awesome times.

Eric Hughes did really well with Saints after Mike, but he took over a young side who were just starting to hit top form when sadly he was replaced. He deserves credit for building that side that went on to be possibly one of the best and most successful in the history of St Helens.

Then came Shaun McRae, a lovely man and great coach, who brought some Aussies in, like Brett Goldspink and many other signings. Both Shaun and Mike had a great sense of humour and instilled a massive family atmosphere and feeling of camaraderie within the club. These, for me, were the best years; I was absolutely blessed to be treated with amazing respect by the players, their families, coaches and board members, not forgetting to mention our amazing loyal spectators, without whom there would be no club.

The fans took me to their hearts and made me feel so welcome and for that I will always be grateful. I worked with some amazing players, coaches and back room staff who will remain lifelong friends. Whenever I go back to Saints to watch I am always made a fuss of and remembered, which is so lovely and so typical of the St Helens people. I am a St Helens girl born and bred yet knew nothing about Saints or rugby league before I joined the club. I'd like to think I know a little more now!

I hope you all enjoy reading what promises to be a great book. Thanks once again, David, for asking me to jot down a few words.

Janette Smith, Physio
July 2020

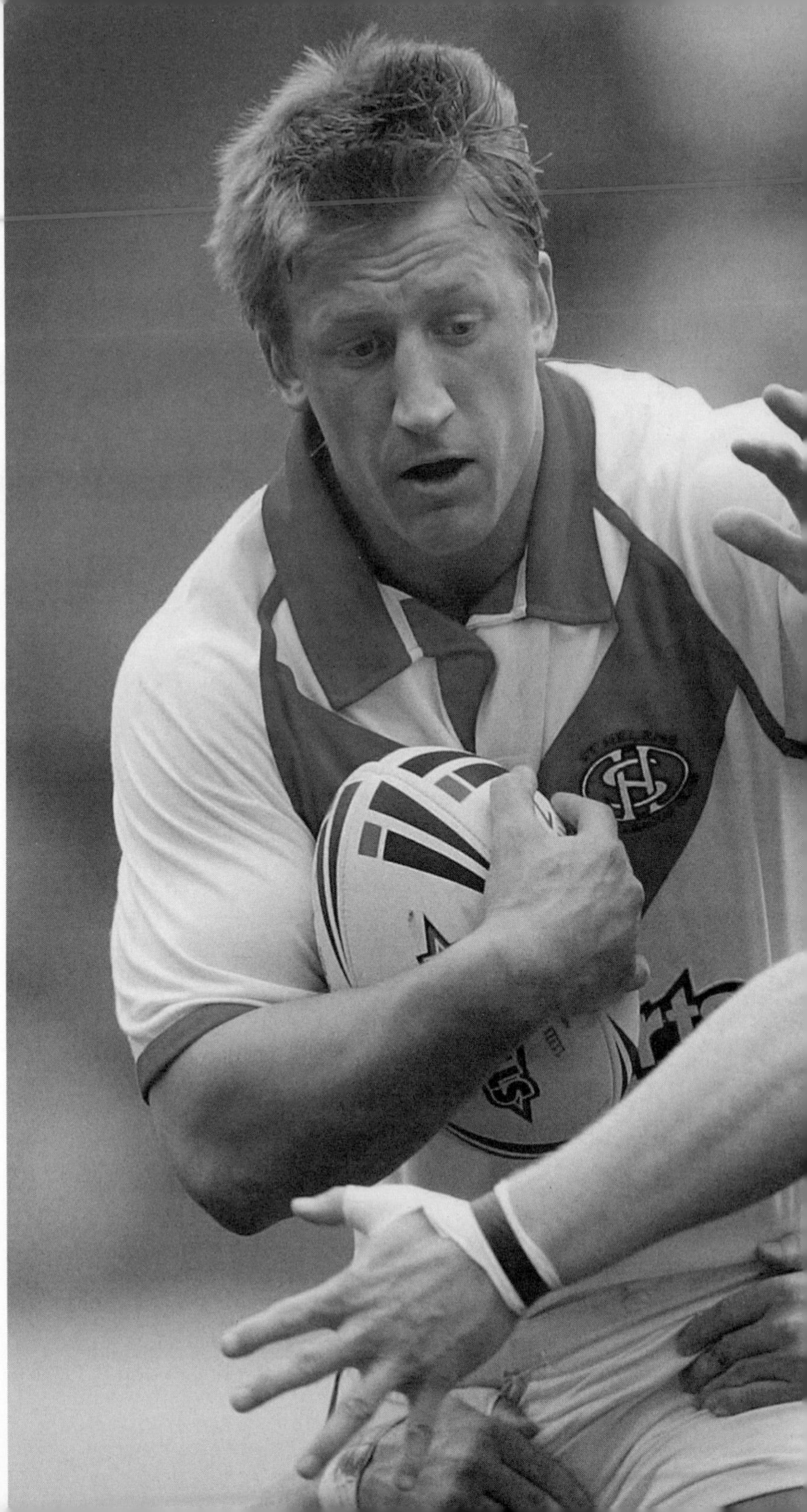

KEITH MASON

Keith Mason

PROP FORWARD 2003–05
HERITAGE NUMBER 1128

BORN: 20 January 1982, Dewsbury

SIGNED: 30 May 2003 from Melbourne Storm

DEBUT: 6 June 2003 vs Wigan Warriors

LAST GAME: 17 September 2005 vs Bradford Bulls

ST HELENS CAREER: 63 appearances (including 25 as a substitute), 4 tries

HONOURS: Challenge Cup 2004, League Leaders' Shield 2005

LEFT: 2005 to join Castleford Tigers

PLAYING CAREER: Wakefield Trinity Wildcats (2000–01), Melbourne Storm (2002–03), St Helens (2003–05), Castleford Tigers (2006), Huddersfield Giants (2006–12), Castleford Tigers (2013)

Keith Mason joined St Helens from Melbourne Storm in May 2003. He made his debut in the red V in a 34-38 home defeat to fierce rivals Wigan Warriors a week later.

The former Dewsbury Moor amateur player was part of the Wakefield Academy before graduating to the first team. His performances for Trinity soon caught the eye of NRL teams and he joined the Melbourne Storm in order to further his career.

Mason left England at the age of 20 to join the Storm and he played four times for them in the NRL; he has since admitted he left a boy and came back a man and he will always be grateful for the time spent in Australia.

During his time at St Helens he scored four tries, but he will be best remembered for his performance in the 2004 Challenge Cup Final against Wigan. Sean Long might have won the Lance Todd Trophy as man of the match, but Mason must have pushed him close with his direct running and strong defence.

A number of injuries curtailed his 2005 campaign and he struggled to hold down a first-team place. He left the Saints and had spells at Castleford Tigers and Huddersfield Giants before calling it a day. Following his retirement, Mason turned his hand to acting and script writing. He has written the first ever comic on rugby league and has plans to spread the name of the sport worldwide.

St Helens 32-16 Wigan Warriors
Challenge Cup Final
Saturday, 15 May 2004
Millennium Stadium, Cardiff
Attendance 73,734

Teams

St Helens	*Wigan Warriors*
Paul Wellens	Kris Radlinski
Ade Gardner	David Hodgson
Martin Gleeson	Sean O'Loughlin
Willie Talau	Kevin Brown
Darren Albert	Brett Dallas
Jason Hooper	Danny Orr
Sean Long	Adrian Lam
Nick Fozzard	Quentin Pongia
Keiron Cunningham	Terry Newton
Keith Mason	Craig Smith
Chris Joynt	Danny Tickle
Lee Gilmour	Gareth Hock
Paul Sculthorpe	Andy Farrell

Subs

Dominic Feaunati	Stephen Wild
Jon Wilkin	Mick Cassidy
Ricky Bibey	Danny Sculthorpe
Mark Edmondson	Terry O'Connor

Coaches

Ian Millward	Mike Gregory

Tries

Gilmour	Newton
Talau (2)	Dallas (2)
Wellens	
Sculthorpe	

Goals

Long (6)	Farrell (2)

Referee: Karl Kirkpatrick

The 2004 Challenge Cup Final was the 103rd time this famous final had been held and it marked the sixth time these clubs were the last two going up against each other.

Before this game kicked off, St Helens had recorded victories over Wigan in 1961 and 1966, while Wigan had beaten the Saints in 1989, 1991 and 2002. After the 80 minutes had been played, the record was now 3-3 and at the time of writing, they have not faced each other in a Challenge Cup Final since.

The Saints were unstoppable during the 2004 Challenge Cup campaign. They started their road to Wembley with a trip to Bradford Bulls in the fourth round and dispatched the cup holders with a convincing 30-10 win at Odsal. In the next round, they played at home against Leeds Rhinos and they advanced to the quarter-finals with a 24-14 success, where they then edged past Hull FC 31-26 to set up a semi-final clash with Huddersfield Giants.

St Helens were unplayable that day and ran out 46-6 winners, then found out they were going to face fierce rivals Wigan in Cardiff as the Warriors had defeated Warrington Wolves 30-18 at Widnes.

Keith Mason admitted that the team he played for in 2004 were a special bunch of players, and they proved that by beating four quality sides on the way to the Challenge Cup Final. On the day in Cardiff, St Helens were too strong for the Warriors and they outscored them five tries to two in a 32-16 victory. Mason revealed it was a boyhood dream to play in a Challenge Cup Final and says he will never forget his time with St Helens, while he goes into detail about his friendship with movie star Mickey Rourke, and the amazing plans he has for the future, which could provide much needed publicity for the sport of rugby league.

I signed for Saints in 2003 from Melbourne Storm. when I came over, I think there had already been 11 or so games in the league and my debut game was on a Friday against Wigan. It was quite a tense game to be thrown straight into, but I loved my time at St Helens, it was just brilliant. We had a bit of success there as well, winning the Challenge Cup Final against Wigan.

That final against Wigan, I would have to say that is one of the best games I have played in during my whole career. Not just for the game itself, but the way we actually reached the final was kind of special too. We had to play pretty much all the form teams in the country before even getting to the final, which is pretty unheard of when you are playing in a competition like the Challenge Cup. You tend to get one or two easier rounds before going up against the big boys.

We played against Bradford Bulls first off and were pretty much written off in that one, with them being the Challenge Cup holders and reigning Super League champions; then we played Leeds Rhinos before having to face off against Hull in the quarter-finals. Then we played Huddersfield Giants in the semi-finals, Huddersfield were playing well that year. Ultimately, we made it to the final against Wigan, in what is probably the biggest derby in rugby league.

That was a really special moment for us as a team. To just get to that final, considering the route we were handed and how hard it was to get there, that is a special achievement. We finally got there in front of a full crowd at the Millennium Stadium in Cardiff and to win it was a boyhood dream of mine come true. The game was in Cardiff because Wembley was being rebuilt, but that didn't take the gloss off it.

I remember the week leading up to the final, I mean obviously the team we had back then was amazing. We had Sean Long at half-back and Jason Hooper had an outstanding season, then we had Darren Albert on the wing and Willie Talau in the centre, also don't forget we had Paul Wellens at full-back.

Then in the forwards we had me, Nick Fozzard, Keiron Cunningham, Chris Joynt, Lee Gilmour, Paul Sculthorpe and the likes of Mark Edmondson coming through as well. I was a young kid; I was only 22 years of age. We went down a few days before, on Wednesday or Thursday, and stayed near Cardiff. We were so relaxed and I just felt so confident and for a young man playing at prop in such a fantastic team, although I was about to play in a massive final, I never really felt any pressure.

It was like a dream come true for me to just get to the final, all the hard work I had put in as a kid, who wasn't really supposed to make it, flying to Australia and then St Helens coming in for me. Basically, it was a dream come true for me to go to the NRL at first and play with Melbourne and then it was another dream come true to play for St Helens in such a talented team.

The good thing about St Helens is that we enjoyed each other's company and we enjoyed the football. It's probably the most I've enjoyed my rugby league, to be fair, in my whole career and that was really down to the talent in the team and how good we were.

On the day of the game it felt so relaxed, we were all just chilled out and ready to go. We went to the stadium the day before. It's an unbelievable stadium, we went in and it was empty obviously, but the next day when we walked out it was packed full of people and it was just amazing. To actually play Wigan in a final like that and go on to beat them was brilliant, but coming out of that tunnel knowing my family, my mum and people who loved me were up in the stands watching me – I felt proud. Not many people go on to win Challenge Cup Finals, so I felt very privileged.

When I was out there playing, I just had a feeling at the beginning of the game that I'd done all the hard work and I was ready and I was fit and I was going to get over my opposite number, which was Quentin Pongia and Craig Smith. I think I did my job. To be honest with you in a game like that it feels like everything is in slow motion. There may have been 80,000 people watching the game in the stadium, but it's a weird feeling, a lot of players will tell you, you are so locked in the game you forget everything around you. The atmosphere was just amazing and we topped it off by winning it.

I remember I made a break early in the first half, I gave an offload to Keiron Cunningham, but Ian Millward took me off in the first half and then brought me back on again. When I came back on, I can remember the ball going through a few pairs of hands. It went through Jason Hooper's hands, Scully, Willie Talau, Lee Gilmour and then Scully back to me again. Wigan captain Andy Farrell came across to take me out and I just tipped it on to Wello [Paul Wellens] to put him under the posts. I think that try was a killer blow to Wigan, I think they were ten points down then or a try down, something like that, but that made it two or three tries ahead and we were in control just before half-time. That really hurt them and set us on course to lift the trophy.

I really enjoyed the final – it was fantastic, just amazing to be part of something like the Challenge Cup Final. I believe I contributed well in the game. I think overall I came third in the ratings for the man of the match – the Lance Todd Trophy. I think Longy [Sean Long] won it that year and Willie Talau was second. It was just fantastic; I remember the final hooter going at the end and Sean Long coming over to me and jumping in my arms. It's something I will never forget, I'm very grateful and blessed to have gone and won a final of that magnitude against a world class team in Wigan. Actually, it was two world-class teams going at it that day and I think we were just that little bit more clinical than they were.

That game gave me a lot of confidence for the rest of my life; it has made me go out on a limb. If there is an opportunity, I just go out there and grab it with both hands and that's what we did as a team that day. We all had parts to play in that game and we all did our jobs very well. We stuck by each other and we got the win; it wasn't an easy Challenge Cup Final. I can remember going and picking up the trophy. I was stood near to Keiron Cunningham and when I lifted that trophy, it was just a surreal moment. It was such an amazing day. We came back for a homecoming and some of the players were more than worse for wear. The coach trip on the way back was probably more memorable than the game itself and that's saying something, you know. But they are memories that will last forever in my mind. I'm still good friends with a lot of the guys from that team and I always will be.

I really enjoyed my time at St Helens. I signed in 2003 as a young prop at 21 years old. I went to Australia as a boy and I came back a man. I really enjoyed my time with Melbourne, but I loved it at St Helens. Knowsley Road was one of the best stadiums I've ever played in and ever will; unfortunately it's gone now but I was glad I was there at that time and in that era. I feel very grateful to have won something with St Helens and to have carved my name into history.

I honestly loved my time at St Helens. I would like to have stayed a lot longer but a new coach came in and I wasn't part of his plans, but that was never going to derail my career. I went on to have seven good years at Huddersfield, and I finished off at Castleford Tigers and I got to play for my country as well.

I'd never been involved in a derby game as such before I signed for St Helens. I came back from Australia and landed on the Saturday before going to watch Saints versus Warrington on the Sunday. You've got to remember at this time in 2003 St Helens had a great team; Darren Britt was starting at prop, Scully had won the Man of Steel twice and Keiron Cunningham was coming back from his injury. Coach Ian Millward just decided to put me straight in. They were struggling with front-rowers and he offered me a deal and I came back for three and a half years.

We were playing Wigan and I obviously knew the rivalry the two had with each other, but I suppose I didn't really know the magnitude of the rivalry. I knew it was a derby and to be honest I didn't have too much time to think about it before my debut. The boys were saying before the game, 'It's a massive match, Keith, and you are going to really enjoy it.' That night, there must have been over 20,000 people at Knowsley Road and it was a red-hot evening and I thought, 'This is brilliant, wow this is fantastic, I've never played in front of a crowd like this before.' It was good to just get thrown in the deep end really as they say. I've played in some cracking derbies against Wigan and I'm actually going to go out and say it is the biggest derby in rugby league. I believe I can say that because I played in it.

During my career, I was lucky enough to play in three Challenge Cup Finals. In 2009 I made the final with Huddersfield Giants and we had a really good year that year. I think I got player of the year and the club's Man of Steel award at their annual dinner, so it was a good year personally.

Going ahead to my relationship with Mickey Rourke, this happened while I was at Huddersfield. We had played Warrington in the Challenge Cup Final in 2009. We had a few players who were a little bit inexperienced and we made too many errors. Warrington capitalised on that and they went on to lift the trophy. That game was another actual boyhood dream of mine because it was played at Wembley. A lot of my childhood memories were at Wembley and I remember going there to watch Great Britain in 1994 when Jonathan Davies scored a try to beat Australia, so for me to play on that pitch was fantastic.

We were at the Park Lane Hotel, my mum and my son were there with me. I can remember Shamu being there. Shamu was a friend and he got us an invite to Stringfellows – the strip club in London. Myself, Scott

Moore and a few other players went down to the hotel bar and I can remember Kris Radlinski was there and Danny Orr, there were a few Wigan players there. Mickey Rourke walked past me, this was in 2009 and he had just made *The Wrestler* movie. It was his comeback film, and I saw him and said, 'That's Mickey Rourkex.' The rest of the team were like, 'Who?'

Obviously, none of them knew who he was; he was a kind of old-school actor, but to me I was like 'Wow, that's Mickey Rourke, *The Wrestler*.' I asked his bodyguard could I say hello to him, he said 'sure, go ahead'. So, I went up to him and I shook his hand, he was sat down and I had this suit on, the Challenge Cup Final suit. I said 'Hiya Mickey, nice to meet you. I really enjoyed your movie *The Wrestler*, is that like a comeback movie for you of your life?' He looked at me like I was strange, and said 'Yeah, pretty much man. What are you, a gangster, an athlete?' I went 'No, no, I'm a rugby player Mickey, in fact I played today at Wembley.' He then said 'I fucking love rugby, in fact I watched you today at Wembley. Great, listen kid, take my number and let's link up.'

It was so strange, one minute I'm talking to him and the next he's giving me his number. So, to cut a long story short, I got his number and a couple of weeks later, when I was at the awards night at Huddersfield – I'd just won pretty much all the awards that night which I was very grateful for – he sent me a message inviting me to the GQ Awards and told me to write these details down. Basically, what he did was, he paid for a hotel for me in Knightsbridge to go down there as his guest to the GQ Awards, which was an annual event for all the celebrities. I went down there with Scott Moore and I took my shirt from the Challenge Cup Final and I threw it at him [Rourke] as he came out of the elevator. He had just won the 'Man of the Year' award, Jason Statham had presented it to him. I gave him my shirt, which had 'Mason' on the back. He was there with Guy Ritchie and it was simply crazy.

We just became friends from there; he invited me over to New York to see him and stay at his place. He invited me over to Beverly Hills, it was just a friendship. Something different for me, from my background. It was quite surreal, but he is just a down to earth guy. I think he liked me because I was a sportsman, he had a lot of time for sportsmen, he doesn't really respect actors in that sense. So, I think that's where his boxing background comes into it. Over the years, every time he would come to England I'd go to London and we'd link up. I'd go to TV shows with him, I went to *The Jonathan Ross Show* with him, which I think had David Beckham and Jackie Chan on there.

Then we got together and wrote a script called *The Welshman* which I helped him with; it was going to be about Gareth Thomas, the former rugby player who is gay. Mickey was interested in doing a life story on him.

I was helping with the script, but it never really got off the ground because Mickey wanted to play someone who was 36 years old and obviously Mickey was in his sixties. It was a crazy time; he took a lot of time out for me and I'll always be grateful for that.

I had a highly publicised court case which I ended up winning against Huddersfield. Mickey rang me a week later and said, 'Hey kid, how are you doing?' I said 'Yeah, I'm good, I've just won my case.' He said, 'Listen, I'm in London next week, I'm shooting a film. I'd like, you to play my bodyguard in the film, can you make it? Can you come and do a screen test?' I'm like 'Sure Mickey.' So, I went down to London and ended up doing a film shoot, which ended up being a speaking role. It was a film called *Skin Traffik (A Hitman in London)*; basically, Mickey opened the door for me into the acting world, which I have been pursuing ever since.

He allowed me to have the screen test and I got the part. Since then I have learned to screen-write and I have brought out the first ever rugby league comic in history. This is going to be massive, also I will be doing *Rugby Blood* the film. I am just finishing the script on that, and I'm in talks with Pinewood Studios. For me as an actor, I want to learn. I don't want to be a good actor, I want to be a great actor. I've been learning about directors, producers, screen writers and being able to sell and distribute a film. All these things I have picked up in the last few years. I've done about seven or eight films now and I've done some TV work as well.

I've got a lot of things planned. *Rugby Blood* the comic is the actual prequel to the film. It tells the story about David King, the main character, he's a rugby league star and entrepreneur. The Russians spot him playing a game of rugby and he's worth a lot of money. What they do is, they use him as a target to take his wife for ransom to get a lot of money out of him. He goes to Monte Carlo on a trip and his wife is kidnapped. He then has to hunt down the bad guys and save his wife. It's basically like rugby league meets James Bond and it's going to be fun.

I've also just finished writing a TV pilot called *Players*, which is about an agent for rugby players. The stuff I have been doing is very original, most of the stuff is what I have experienced myself. Whether I am acting or writing, I am putting my own experiences into each project. Having played at Super League and NRL level for 14 years, I can add quite a lot. In *Players* the TV pilot, I am dealing with a lot of underlying issues in the game, whether it's drugs, pain-killers or players getting sacked. It's got a lot of drama in it as well. I'm just getting my fingers in a lot of pies at the minute in the film industry.

Watch this space.

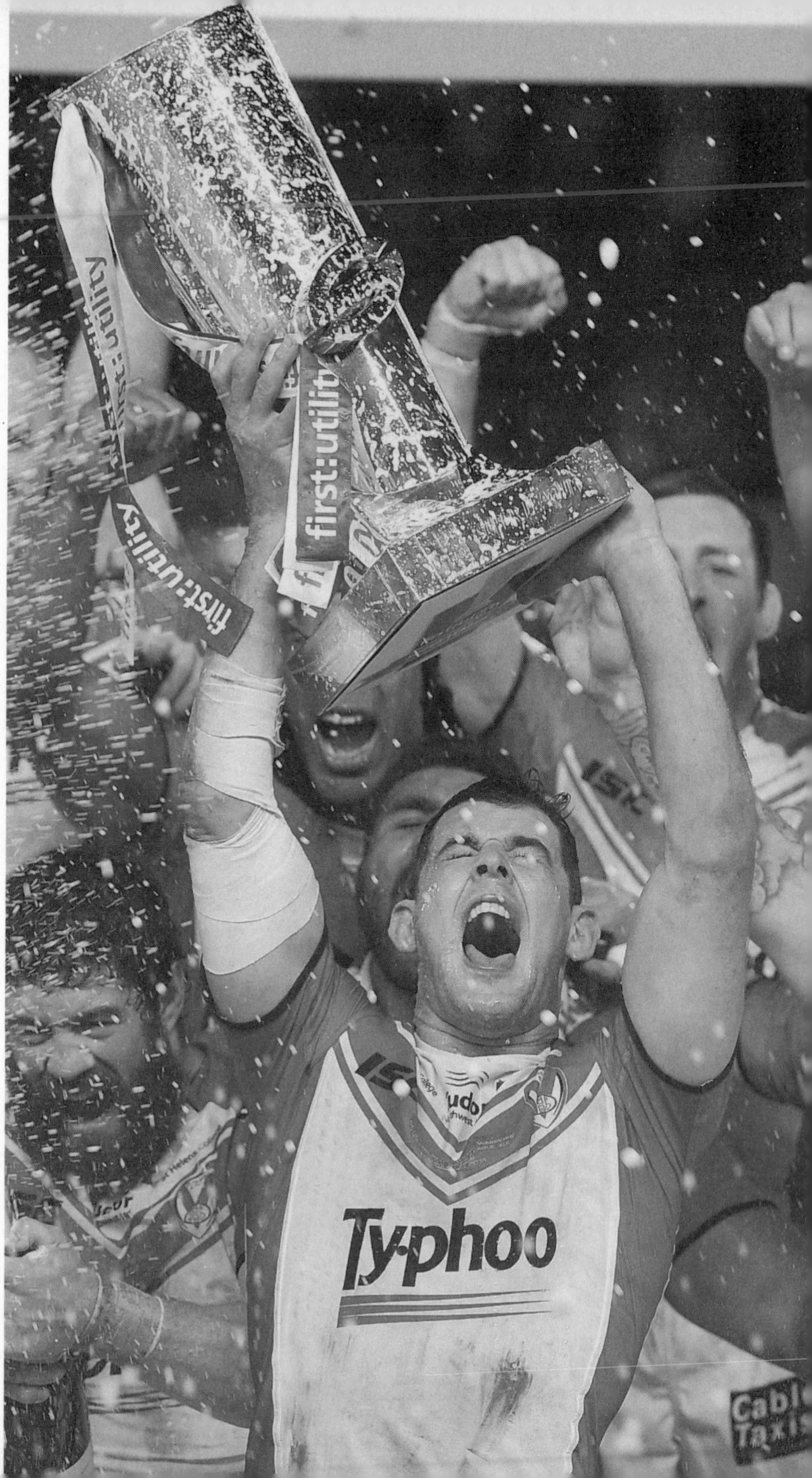
first:utility
Typhoo

Paul Wellens

FULL-BACK 1998–2015
HERITAGE NUMBER 1087

BORN: 27 February 1980, St Helens

SIGNED: 3 June 1998 from Blackbrook

DEBUT: 30 August 1998 vs Halifax Blue Sox

LAST GAME: 31 March 1996 vs Workington Town

ST HELENS CAREER: 495 appearances (including 44 as a substitute), 231 tries, 40 goals, 1 drop goal

HONOURS: Super League 1999, 2000, 2002, 2006, 2014; World Club Challenge 2001, 2007; Challenge Cup 2001, 2004, 2006, 2007, 2008; Man of Steel 2006

LEFT: Retired in 2015

PLAYING CAREER: St Helens (1998–2015)

It wouldn't be unfair or disrespectful to the past players of St Helens to say that Paul Wellens is the real 'Mr St Helens'. In all my time covering rugby league, I have never heard a bad word said against him and he has always been available when I have needed his help.

Wellens joined St Helens as a youngster when he was trying his hand at both rugby league and union. Luckily for our sport, St Helens came calling first and he started playing for the academy side. He may have been a fresh-faced youngster when he made his debut in 1998 against Halifax, but he soon showed everyone he had an old head on young shoulders.

Wellens played just under 500 games for his home-town club and St Helens was the only professional club he ever played for. During his time with the Saints, he won everything on offer. He is a five-time Super League Grand Final winner, he has won the Challenge Cup five times and the World Club Challenge twice.

As well as winning five Grand Finals, Wellens was also part of the St Helens squad that lost five consecutive Grand Finals from 2007–11. He now admits that, contrary to what he said in numerous press interviews in the lead-up to the 2014 Grand Final – the game he has chosen in this book – those defeats were very much on his mind ahead of that game against Wigan.

The Grand Final hoodoo was put to rest on that day in 2014 and it was one of the proudest moments of Wellens' career as he led his home-town team out at Old Trafford as captain and then went on to lift the Super League trophy.

Wellens' career was cut short in April 2015 with his final game coming in a 12-4 defeat at Wigan. He couldn't continue playing with pain-killing injections if he was going to live a full life after his career was over. So, he made the decision to retire and for the benefit of his health, he knows it was the correct option.

St Helens 14-6 Wigan Warriors

Super League Grand Final
Saturday, 11 October 2014
Old Trafford, Manchester
Attendance 70,102

Teams

St Helens	*Wigan Warriors*
Paul Wellens	Matty Bowen
Tommy Makinson	Josh Charnley
Mark Percival	Anthony Gelling
Josh Jones	Dan Sarginson
Adam Swift	Joe Burgess
Mark Flanagan	Blake Green
Lance Hohaia	Matty Smith
Kyle Amor	Ben Flower
James Roby	Sam Powell
Mose Masoe	Dom Crosby
Louie McCarthy-Scarsbrook	Joel Tomkins
Sia Soliola	Liam Farrell
Jordan Turner	Sean O'Loughlin

Subs

Willie Manu	Eddy Pettybourne
Alex Walmsley	Tony Clubb
Greg Richards	John Bateman
Luke Thompson	George Williams

Coaches

Nathan Brown	Shaun Wane

Tries

Soliola	Burgess
Makinson	

Goals

Percival (3)	Smith

Referee: Phil Bentham

Wellens has chosen the 2014 Super League Grand Final against Wigan Warriors as his favourite game in a St Helens shirt. He admits it is special for more than one reason and finally helped lay a few Grand Final ghosts to rest.

This game will always be remembered for the incident in the second minute when Wigan prop Ben Flower was deservedly sent off for punching Saints stand-off Lance Hohaia off the ball. A lot has been made of that incident since and we don't need to go into it here, but Wellens felt the sending-off spurred Wigan on and he admits St Helens had to dig really deep in order to leave Manchester as champions.

A strong second half performance for the Saints, with tries from Sia Soliola and Tommy Makinson, saw them record their sixth Super League title and their first since beating Hull FC 26-4 in 2006. You could see the delight and relief on the face of Wellens and what it meant to him to lead his home-town team to glory.

In this chapter, Wellens also goes on to remember the day he went from being a cheering spectator at Knowsley Road to sharing a changing room and field with the likes of Vila Matautia, Paul Newlove, Anthony Sullivan, Sean Long, Keiron Cunningham, Apollo Perelini and Paul Sculthorpe.

It's quite difficult to come up with one stand-out game considering the amount I played for St Helens, but I would have to go with the most recent success. So, that would be the 2014 Grand Final game against Wigan at Old Trafford.

It was memorable for a number of reasons really, but I think more so because I was captain that day as well. To captain your home-town team in a Grand Final makes it special and puts it up there with one of the best things we did.

It was kind of a funny season for us to be honest; we started it off really well at the start of 2014 and then we ended up picking up a lot of injuries. We lost the likes of Jon Wilkin, Luke Walsh – not just key players, but key players in key positions. We went into that Grand Final, and for want of a better word, we had a lot of square pegs in round holes. I think we ended up finishing that game with Mark Flanagan and myself in the halves. Lance Hohaia started the game and obviously he went off after the Ben Flower incident, but it was one of the occasions where it was an all-hands-on-deck mentality. We knew that we were missing some influential players and we probably didn't have a lot of points in us that day. We had to back our defence really, and everyone to a man did that.

Although it probably should have made it a little easier for us with the sending-off at the beginning of the game, that didn't really happen. Sometimes, and I've been in these situations myself, there are teams that have gone down to 12 men and it actually galvanises you a little bit and brings that five or ten per cent extra out of everybody that you probably didn't know was there. I think that happened that day with Wigan. Sean

O'Loughlin was the captain and Shaun Wane was head coach. They have shown before that day and since that they have an unbelievably competitive nature about what they can deliver. So, by no means did I look at that sending-off and think that makes it a foregone conclusion, because we still had to, during periods of that game, hang in there and do it tough because Wigan kept coming and coming at us, just like we envisaged they would.

I do think that incident, although they lost a man in Ben Flower, it caused a lot of disruption for us as well, in terms that Lance Hohaia left the field and I reverted to stand-off with Tommy Makinson leaving the wing to go to full-back, while Louie McCarthy-Scarsbrook moved to the centres. So yeah, it caused us some disruption as well. That's why I have already said that we were probably not going to have that creativity or everything that Saints are renowned for; we had to find a different way to win.

One thing we did that day, was that we controlled the ball really well. I think we hardly made any errors, but at half-time we were behind and it's very easy when you are losing to a team as good as Wigan and they are down to 12 men, you can kind of implode a little bit and get frustrated. One thing we managed to do that day was really keep our composure and keep competing. We knew that it wasn't going to be one of those games where we would score 20 or 30 points, I don't think either side were going to do that, so we knew we just had to be patient and work out our opportunities and take them whenever they came. I think it was a real strong carry from Sia Soliola to score a try which put us in front, and from that moment on I think the onus was on them to kind of chase the game a little bit. The way that we were defending – not just that game, but in the play-off games previously – there was a real solidarity about the way we defended, and it shone through on that day as well.

When that final whistle went, you can see what it meant to me. It was probably more than just one game for me, to be honest with you. I think there was only myself and James Roby in the squad that day that had played in five successive Grand Final defeats from 2007 until 2011. In the build-up to that game as captain, I was asked a lot of questions in press conferences about, 'Do you think about those Grand Final losses and does it affect you?' I basically lied through my teeth all week. I was saying 'I don't really think about it, it's not something I dwell on', but to be truthful it is something I thought about day in, day out. I couldn't go public with that because I didn't want my team-mates in and around me to feel the same kind of pressure I was feeling. We kind of got into a habit of going to Old Trafford and coming away on the wrong side of things, I understand that too, but a lot of those players in that squad had not gone through the same things we had. As they were going into it in a healthy state of mind, why would they be thinking about games they hadn't be involved in in the past? So it was just a case of keeping everyone on an even footing with a clear thought process on what needed to be done in that game.

For me personally, it was probably a lot about avenging those five Grand Final defeats, finally getting back there to win one. I think it takes a fair bit of courage as a team, when you have had so many disappointments, to keep going back and keep challenging yourself and we did that on that day.

I've been retired a few years now and I can look back on my career instead of dwelling on the fact I'm not playing anymore. It was just an unbelievable experience, to go from watching them on the terraces to playing in the first team and to play with all those players that only 12 months before I was stood cheering on. I built so many relationships and played with so many great players, at a club where, despite what is happening, the expectations are that you will win and be competing. You go to Challenge Cup Finals and Grand Finals; that's what I really enjoyed about it the most, that regardless of how successful you were the year before, or whether you didn't win anything, every year you would get on the starting blocks and there would be an expectation around the club to win and that's what made it all exciting.

I was at Blackbrook Royals for a bit and I also played rugby union at a club called West Park. I was kind of flitting between the two before I signed for St Helens. I remember getting a phone call saying would I go down and train with the St Helens academy and I had a few training sessions and played at the weekend, things then started to take shape a little bit. I enjoyed it and I found my feet and things progressed from there. My debut was under Shaun McRae at the back end of 1998. I was actually at college at the time and I got a phone call from Mike Gregory – who was Shaun's assistant – and he asked would I come up to training, and when I got to training I didn't expect to be playing, I just thought they might have needed a few extra numbers. When they told me I was going to be on the bench that weekend, I was absolutely made up.

I remember my debut as well. It was against Halifax. I was a scrum-half at the time playing in the juniors and I came off the bench playing at scrum-half to replace Sean Long. Looking back now, it was probably a wise move that I switched to full-back because displacing Sean Long in that St Helens team would have been a really difficult task.

The fans have been great with me. All of my adult life I have been a Saints player so I was in and around the town and I have become quite used to talking with the public about rugby, it wasn't something that I shied away from. Whether it be down the local shop or in pubs or clubs, people wanted to talk about rugby and I always bought into that really. Along the way, there would be people who would voice their discontent at times when things weren't going well, but I always saw that, in some respects, as a bit of a positive. Like I said before, there is an expectation to win when you play for St Helens, I think the flip side is to play at a club where people slap you on the back for mediocrity. I don't think you would ever want that, and certainly the St Helens public don't want that and as players you should embrace the fact that you are under pressure to perform week in, week out.

Deep down, you know when it's time to call it a day. In my mind, I was thinking of retiring at the back end of the 2015 season, but 18 months previous I had started having problems with my hip, very similar to the one that Andy Murray went through. When you see the news with him on, I can see the same symptoms. I was having steroid injections in it to try and keep me on the field in training and in games, but those injections have a depreciating effect as well, by my third or fourth injection they weren't taking any effect whatsoever. It just became worse and worse, so that it got to the point where my quality of life was very poor.

It became not really about training and playing rugby, it was just about getting my quality of life back and that's when I made the decision to call time on things and get the operation I needed doing. It was a difficult decision, but I have no doubts that it was the right one. It kind of put my mind at ease really. If you had told me at 18 that I would retire at 35 and play for all those years I would have bitten your hand off, so, although it was disappointing at the time not finishing the season, you have to look at it in a certain way and there are certainly a lot of positives I can take away from my career. The back end, the way it finished, that's just the way it is, it's part and parcel of the game sometimes that you don't always get what you want, but by no means am I overly disappointed by it.

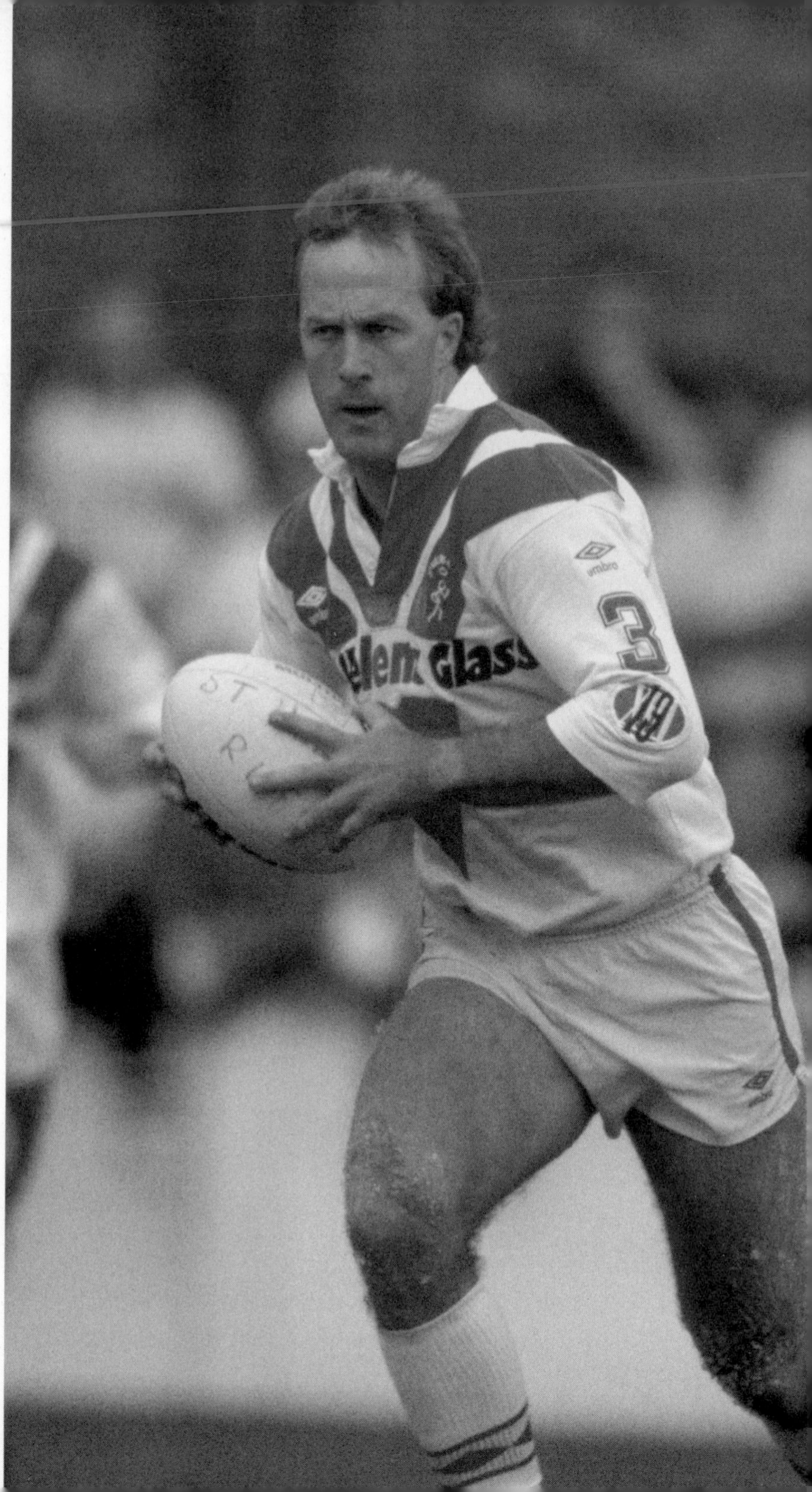

PHIL VEIVERS

Phil Veivers

FULL-BACK 1984–1996
HERITAGE NUMBER 970

BORN: 25 May 1964, Beaudesert, Queensland

SIGNED: 24 June 1984 from Brisbane Souths

DEBUT: 7 October 1984 vs Castleford Tigers

LAST GAME: 31st March 1996 vs Workington Town

ST HELENS CAREER: 381 appearances (including 49 as a substitute), 98 tries, 5 drop goals

HONOURS: Lancashire Cup 1984, 1992; John Player Trophy 1988; Premiership Trophy 1985, 1993

LEFT: 1996 to join Huddersfield Giants

PLAYING CAREER: St Helens (1984–96), Huddersfield Giants (1996–98)

COACHING CAREER: Salford Red Devils (2011–13), Workington Town (2014–16)

Phil Veivers is one of a long line of players who was an unknown quantity when he first signed for St Helens, but like many more after him, he left a club legend.

Veivers was not the first-choice signing that Saints had their eye on in 1984. They had already agreed to sign Mal Meninga, while they were hoping to sign full-back Gary Belcher. Belcher ended up not joining St Helens as he didn't want to sign for a full season, so they turned their attention to Veivers and after speaking to the great Wayne Bennett, he decided to give it a go and spend 12 months in the United Kingdom, before returning home to Australia.

At the time of writing, the year is 2020 and Phil Veivers is still living in the north-west of England and is fully settled with his wife and kids. That was a long 12 months, wasn't it?

Veivers loved his time at St Helens and ended up winning the Lancashire Cup in his first season despite getting injured early on in the win over Wigan. He also lifted the Premiership on two occasions, the John Player Special Trophy and the Lancashire Cup one more time during his time at Knowsley Road.

Veivers played in an era that was dominated by Wigan, and he has chosen a very special win over Saints' biggest rivals on their own turf of Central Park. Veivers admits that he didn't know how big the rivalry was with Wigan until a number of spectators approached him one day on the way to the changing rooms at Knowsley Road.

Veivers would have loved to have been a one-club man, but he explains what happened in his final days as a Saints player before being offloaded to Huddersfield Giants.

Wigan Warriors 22-32 St Helens
Stones Bitter Championship
Sunday, 27 December 1987
Central Park, Wigan
Attendance 23,809

Teams

Wigan Warriors	*St Helens*
Steve Hampson	Phil Veivers
David Marshall	Kevin McCormack
Joe Lydon	Paul Loughlin
Ellery Hanley	Mark Elia
Kevin Iro	Les Quirk
Shaun Edwards	Shane Cooper
Andy Gregory	Neil Holding
Ian Lucas	Tony Burke
Martin Dermott	Paul Groves
Brian Case	Peter Souto
Graeme West	Paul Forber
Ian Potter	Roy Haggerty
Andy Goodway	Andy Platt

Subs

Richard Russell	Dave Tanner
Adrian Shelford	Stuart Evans

Coaches

Graham Lowe	Alex Murphy

Tries

Lydon 2	Veivers 2
Iro	McCormack
Goodway	Tanner
	Quirk

Goals

Lydon (3)	Loughlin (6)

Referee: John Holdsworth

The game Veivers has chosen as his most memorable was a victory the day after Boxing Day in 1987 at Central Park against Wigan – the win was so memorable because the Saints were so far behind at half-time, they had seemingly no chance of winning.

Well, they did win. And not only that, they kept Wigan scoreless in the second half. Wigan were 22-6 up at the break and looked in full control thanks to a brace of tries from Joe Lydon and one each from Kevin Iro and Andy Goodway.

Saints appeared to be dead and buried and it looked like Wigan would run up a cricket score. Coach Alex Murphy gave his players both barrels at half-time and they came out and were more determined than Wigan and totally outplayed them.

Veivers helped himself to a brace of tries – one of them resulted in a penalty try and the other he has since admitted was a knock on. But no one at St Helens cared, as further tries from David Tanner and Les Quirk saw them complete an amazing comeback – one which some Saints fans still talk about to this day.

In this chapter, Veivers explains that he only ever planned on playing in England for 12 months and never for one moment did he think he would be the only Australian to be awarded a testimonial match at St Helens. He also goes into detail about the disappointment of missing out on a Challenge Cup winners' medal after being overlooked for the final against Bradford Bulls in 1996.

The game I always have to pick was in 1987 when we came back from 22-6 at Central Park against Wigan. I will always pick this one.

I remember we were getting hammered at half-time, nothing seemed to go right for us at all in that first 40 minutes. Wigan seemed to play at a high level and basically controlled the game for the first half. Murph [Alex Murphy] did his nut and shouted at a few people, bollocked a few more and sorted a few things out. Then we came out a different beast in the second half.

I remember we knew we had to score first to have any chance, and Platty [Andy Platt] made half a break, I backed him up on the outside and got an offload and as I went in to score, Graeme West came across and raised his arm and caught me. I did the dying swan, laid down as if I'd been shot by a bazooka. Platty came running over, saying, 'Are you alright, are you alright?' I just winked at him and said, 'Yeah, cool, don't worry about it.' We ended up getting an eight point try for that one, and that got us back in the game at 22-14 and we went on from there.

It was a case of us gaining more and more in confidence. I don't know if I was the next scorer or someone else might have scored the next try. I remember Shane Cooper came in on the last play and put a little kick through, I think I have watched it back and I actually knocked the ball on to be fair, as I tried to pick it up, but it wasn't given and I went on and scored a second try. That score then put us in front and then we scored another try late on and we won 32-22.

They had a pretty high-quality side that day, and for us to roll them over after they got into a pretty commanding lead was a special feat to say the least. I had a pretty fair game on that day, I created a try for Dave Tanner as well as scoring the two tries, so yeah you don't get to go to Wigan's home ground too many times around Christmas time and go that many points down and come away with a win.

We didn't really change anything tactically. I think it was a case of we went out flat in the first half and they got a bit of a roll on us to start with. I think during that year, we were pretty known for being slow starters and then finishing big. What really changed was our mentality, I believe – we spoke at half-time that we had under achieved in the first half and we had nothing to lose really, so we agreed that we needed to step up the pace a bit and play with a bit more flair, and get the offloads out, try and create some space with second-phase ball. There were plenty of offloads from Andy Platt that day and it actually worked out for us in the end.

Regarding my move to St Helens, I don't think I was on St Helens' radar before they signed me. Saints went out to Australia to sign Mal Meninga, and a full-back. They actually went out to sign Gary Belcher, but they gave the job to Ray French and he was out there commentating on the Great Britain Ashes tour. So, Frenchy had come to Souths to watch a game and he'd spoken to Mal and Gary, but Gary wasn't willing to go for a full season. Then Frenchy contacted John Clegg, I think it was at the time, who was the chairman and said: 'Gary Belcher is not willing to come for a full season, but there is another kid here playing who is very good and I think he can do a job for us.' They then told Frenchy to go and have a word with this kid, and that happened to be me.

He came over and asked me if I was willing to go over to the UK, so I said, 'Give us a few days to think about it so I can speak to a few people.' I spoke to my coach at the time, who was Wayne Bennett. I said, 'Is it worth it going for six months?' and he said, 'Go for 12 months.' I went back to Frenchy and told him I would sign for 12 months and that's how it all started really. Frenchy contacted John Clegg and it went from there.

I came over with Mal on the same plane after we had lost heavily to Wynnum Manly in the Grand Final. I came here to get 12 months' experience, that was the whole point of me coming over here. I was just meant to be here for 12 months and then I would go back to Australia because that was my first full year of first grade football. The year before that, I had set myself a target of playing one game and I played eight games, the second year was to play half a season and I played the full season. So, I thought, 'If I go over to England and play for 12 months and get some experience I can come back and move on from there.' Saints then offered me a two-year deal after my first year was up and I went back to Australia in the off-season for three months to play for Souths again and I broke my thumb in the first game, and when I came back from that injury I dislocated my AC joint in training, so that was a pretty woeful off-season to be fair.

The second year I came back here, it wasn't as successful a season for me because I was carrying a couple of knocks, and I was also carrying some extra weight. I thought I would put some extra weight on to try and play a little bit heavier, but it didn't work for me. I lost the weight and then in my third year I had another good season.

I know I chose the Wigan game as my favourite one for Saints, but before I came over, I didn't know anything about the rivalry. On the day of the first game, which was Castleford at home, in October 1984, I was walking from the car to the changing rooms and I was pretty much told in no uncertain terms that they didn't give a shit how I played or who we beat in the season as long as we beat Wigan on Boxing Day and over Easter on Good Friday. So, that was basically my introduction in how the rivalry was between Wigan and Saints; you could lose every game in the season and as long as you beat Wigan twice, they were happy.

I love the club. I always enjoy going back there. I attend a few past players' dinners and all that and bump into a load of old blokes and we have a good chat about our playing days. Over the years I have got to know some of the guys who came after me – the newest crop. I got to play with Keiron Cunningham. It won't make Keiron feel any younger, but I was there for his debut and he went on to be an absolute superstar for the club. I have got an affiliation with the club obviously, from the time I was there. I played for 12 years, I played 381 games there and ended up doing a testimonial and I think I am the only Australian who ever got a testimonial at St Helens. They are my team, I suppose. Realistically I would have stayed for a couple more years, but the directors at the time felt that when I got past 30, they needed to make money on me, so they put me on the transfer list and put a transfer fee on my head.

I remember the day. I had been playing in that truncated season where they were moving into Super League for summer rugby, my last game was against Workington Town away. The Challenge Cup was still going on and I had played in every game in it. I played in the semi-final and I thought, 'I'm going to Wembley,' and I thought I may as well hang around and see what is happening. Bobbie Goulding then came up to me and said, 'Listen mate, you are best off going and finding another club, because the directors have told Shaun McRae not to pick you, because they want you out of here.' I hung around and even when we got to Wembley there was still a lot of doubt over a number of players. I think there were three players that came back from injury that day, I think there was Simon Booth, Alan Hunte and one more, I think it was Karle Hammond. So, I was 18th man. I still thought I had a chance of playing leading up to the game in the week, so I hung around until after the Challenge Cup Final and then I went to Huddersfield the following weekend. They [Saints] made me play in the A team on the Friday night and I played for Huddersfield on the Sunday, a week after Wembley.

It didn't end the way I wanted it to, I would have loved to have been a one-club man, but it didn't happen that way and I went on to represent Huddersfield and I ended up captaining them up to Super League in 1997. In 1996, Daryl van der Velde was the coach who had brought me in over there, and I enjoyed my time there as well. The second year, Steve Fer4res was the coach and it was a good crew of blokes there and we went on to beat Hull in the Grand Final at Old Trafford to get us in to Super League.

TEA ROPATI

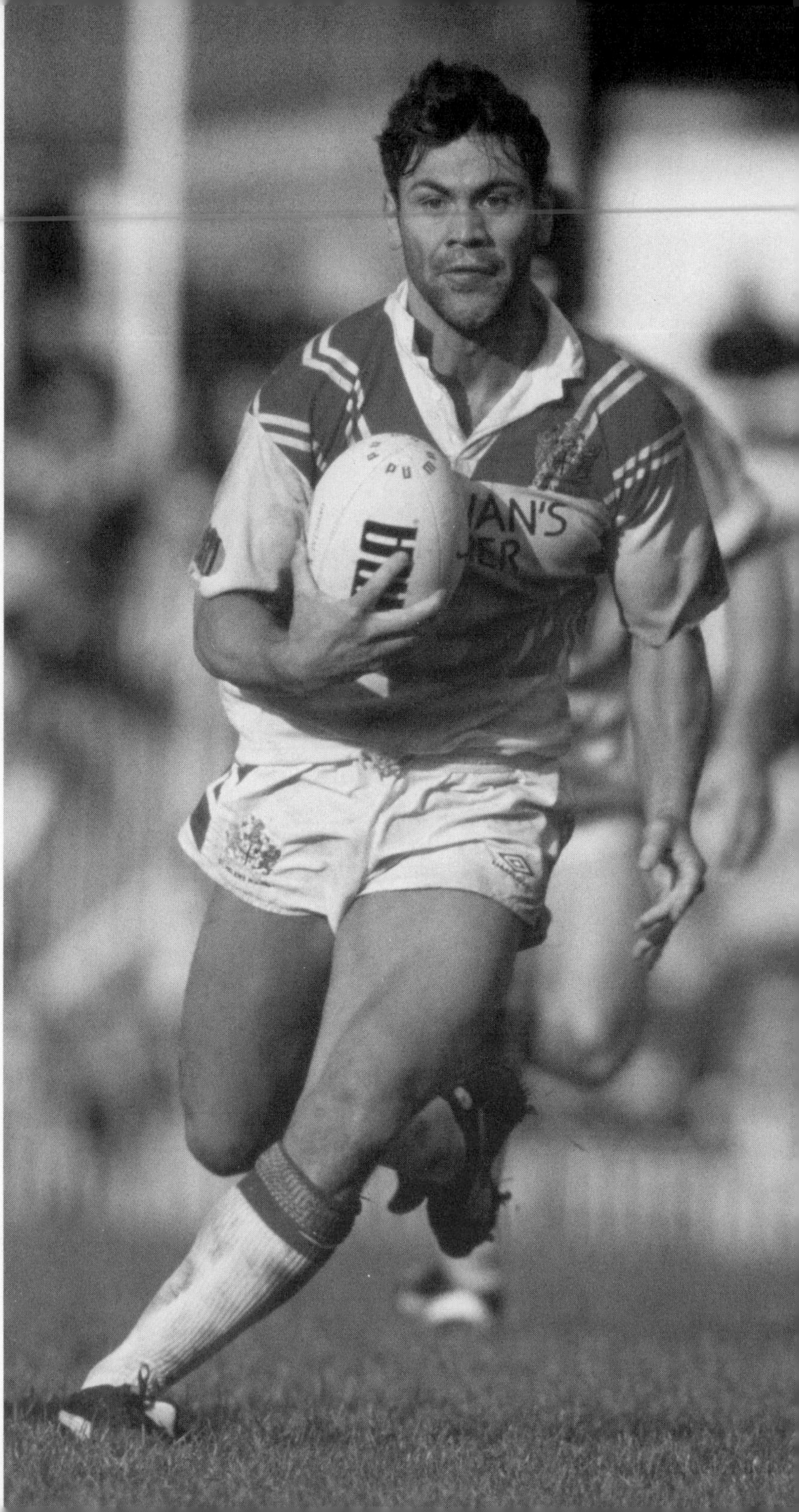

Tea Ropati

CENTRE/STAND-OFF 1989–94
HERITAGE NUMBER 1021

BORN: 7 September 1965, Auckland, New Zealand

SIGNED: 1989 from Mangere East

DEBUT: 13 December 1989 vs Dewsbury

LAST GAME: 8 May 1994 vs Wigan

ST HELENS CAREER: 129 appearances (including 2 as a substitute), 56 tries, 24 goals, 2 drop goals

HONOURS: Lancashire Cup 1991; Premiership Trophy 1993

LEFT: 1994 to join Auckland Warriors

PLAYING CAREER: Newcastle Knights (1988), St Helens (1989–94), Auckland Warriors (1995–98)

Tea Ropati joined St Helens in 1989 and was part of a very talented group of New Zealanders at the club, that included players Shane Cooper and George Mann and, not long afterwards, head coach Mike McClennan.

Ropati was a talented player and could change a game with the blink of an eye, but it is not too harsh to say that St Helens didn't get to see the best of him because of injuries. When he was on the field, he gave 100 per cent and was always willing to do what was best for the team. During his interview for this book, Ropati admitted he didn't know a lot about the rivalry between St Helens and Wigan, but it didn't take him long to become clued up and within weeks he hated them just as if he was born in St Helens.

He has chosen the 1993 Premiership Trophy win at Old Trafford against Wigan as his favourite game, although there are honourable mentions for the 41-6 drubbing of Wigan on Boxing Day and the 1991 Challenge Cup Final at Wembley – for someone who didn't know much about the rivalry, he soon understood that beating Wigan was the be-all and end-all.

He also chose that game because he felt that was the time when they achieved what they had set out to do: to be classed as a very good team. Within a few years, that team had split up but Ropati holds his time in England very close to his heart and will always have a lot of love for the people of St Helens and the club.

St Helens 10-4 Wigan

Premiership Trophy Final
Sunday, 16 May 1993
Old Trafford, Manchester
Attendance 36,598

Teams

St Helens	*Wigan*
Dave Lyon	Paul Atcheson
Mike Riley	Jason Robinson
Gary Connolly	Sam Panapa
Paul Loughlin	Andrew Farrar
Alan Hunte	Martin Offiah
Tea Ropati	Frano Botica
Gus O'Donnell	Shaun Edwards
Jon Neill	Neil Cowie
Bernard Dwyer	Martin Dermott
George Mann	Kelvin Skerrett
Chris Joynt	Mick Cassidy
Sonny Nickle	Andy Farrell
Shane Cooper	Phil Clarke

Subs

Jonathan Griffiths	Ian Gildart
Phil Veivers	Mike Forshaw

Coaches

Mike McClennan	John Monie

Tries

Connolly	Forshaw
Loughlin	

Drop Goals

O'Donnell (2)

Referee: John Holdsworth

St Helens went into the 1993 Premiership Trophy Final at Old Trafford against a Wigan side that had already won the League Championship, Challenge Cup, Regal Trophy and Lancashire Cup. Victory in the Premiership Trophy would have seen them complete the Grand Slam. Well, you can always trust St Helens to spoil a party. And boy, did they do that in Manchester on a rainy Sunday afternoon.

Wigan seemed to roll over everyone in their path in the late eighties and nineties, but Saints always used to push them as close as anyone else. They did more than that in 1993 as they prevented Wigan from playing their free-flowing rugby.

Tries from the soon-to-be-departed Gary Connolly and Paul Loughlin saw the Saints stop Wigan winning the Grand Slam with Gus O'Donnell also dropping two goals to secure a 10-4 win. Before the introduction of Super League, many fans would have said that was their best moment of being a Saints fan.

In this chapter, Ropati reveals that he felt the club lacked ambition in not trying hard enough to keep Gary Connolly at the club. He feels that team would have gone on to be one of the greatest had they kept their best players.

I have got to say that there are so many memorable games I played in during my time with the Saints. With that in mind, I'm going to say that three of them are top of the list as they all mean a lot. The first would probably be the 1992–93 Premiership Trophy win at

Old Trafford. The second game would be the Boxing Day hammering of Wigan in the same season, and lastly the Wembley Challenge Cup Final in 91. Having said that, I will probably focus on the Premiership Trophy win as it kind of tied everything together nicely.

The build-up to the Premiership Trophy Final was memorable as I was actually ruled out two weeks before we played that game. I had torn a rib cartilage and looked like having no chance of playing at all. I think we had a break before the week leading into the match. As I had no chance of being fit, I thought about asking coach Mike McClennan if I could go drink beer and lay on the beach in Tenerife.

Big John Harrison was also injured and agreed that that was a pretty decent kind of plan. I said to Big John that he should go and ask Mike as he was always one of Mike's pets, to which he wanted no part. He quickly reminded me that Mike and I both spoke 'Kiwi' and that I would surely get the outcome we wanted. Reluctantly on behalf of myself and Big John, I knocked on Mike's office door, seeking permission to have a small summer getaway. I suggested it had been a long season and we were of no use to anyone, adding that I felt we would be distracting the lads by hanging around. Furthermore, some salt water and sun would help our recovery and we would both be better for it in the long run.

I thought it was a fairly compelling case that I put forward, especially minus the part involving drinking beers. Mike took some breaking down though – two hours later I had the answer we wanted and the next day we were at Manchester airport on our way to the sun and fun that awaited us. The story got even crazier once we landed in Tenerife. We arrived quite late but managed to find Gary Lineker's bar (he was nowhere to be found which was disappointing) and proceeded to nail a few cold ones. The game plan at this point was to enjoy a few more then wander home for a good night's rest. The walk back to the hotel was interrupted with an obligatory stop at McDonald's where once again I was reminded of the mighty power of the big fella, when I saw him nailing around five burgers. To be totally fair, I wasn't exactly seeing straight so it may well have been only four as we headed across the road to sit down on the beach to feast.

I recall waking in the morning, closer to lunchtime than breakfast, and there were people everywhere – we had fallen asleep on the beach and Big John was burnt to the max. Luckily my Samoan blood allowed for a good old-fashioned tanning and unfortunately for John his face, arms and legs were seriously sunburnt. He spent the next four days sitting in an undersized bath trying to stay cool, only venturing outdoors when the day's sunshine had disappeared. He became nocturnal and I would spend days on the beach without him, where the sand, sun and sea were pure magic. We enjoyed the rest of the break as best we could.

We got back to Knowsley Road and went to training, the lads all looked really good. It should be noted, however, that some of the lads' sun-bed tans didn't quite stand up against what a week in the sun on the beach in Tenerife can do for you. I was feeling pretty good all round to be honest, really refreshed and recharged.

I thought I'd take my kit along and popped into the physio's room to see Janette Smith who was like, 'Hey, how is it feeling? Get up here and let's have a look.' I got on the table and had some treatment and said, 'I might have a bit of a run around with the lads if that's OK?' Janette was, 'Yeah sure, it seems to have improved a bit,' so I'm straight out there and knocking about with a game of touch and pass. I was actually surprised at how good it felt. I had been in a lot of pain when it happened, I couldn't sleep properly and just generally getting about it would hurt like mad. I got through the touch and pass and then the guys were doing some drills which happened to involve tackle contact. I thought 'why not', so I did and then the next thing I know I'm thinking this may be OK! Mike's watching and comes over to me and says, 'Hey, how's it going?' I'm like, 'I think the sea and sun at Tenerife has worked a miracle!' I honestly couldn't believe it as the next thing I knew I was on my way to Old Trafford to play the final.

It was amazing, as at the time I was so disappointed at having to miss such a big match. The boys were all joking around and having me on about faking an injury to get a holiday – Bernard [Dwyer] and Lockers [Paul Loughlin] being the worst of them all. I think between the sun, sea and one of the best physiotherapists I've ever worked with, I was very fortunate.

The week leading up to the game is a little intense, everyone is trying really hard to stay calm and focused but it's hard to not feel that sense of anticipation and excitement. It's a week when best mates feel terribly well connected with one another. The training sessions are more intense than usual and it's also the last game for the season. The group I played with were very tight, we all stuck together and did most things with our wives and girlfriends – we were like one big family.

Having taken the initial jibes from the guys, we got down to business and made sure that we were ready to play. Wardy [Kevin Ward] had also hurt himself pretty badly that year and it played quite heavily on many of our minds. There was some talk about giving the best we could for him but mostly it was internalised by the majority of the group – we knew how much he had given us all and it was time for us to go out and win for him. Wigan were without a few players when their team was announced but to be honest, Wardy, Antony Sullivan and Big John were worth much more to us than what they had lost, so our backs were against the wall.

I remember arriving at the game and, as with all the big matches, there's always that spring in your step. The lads would play cards on the way to matches and there was always loads of laughter and joking about. This trip was no different, although I can recall everyone being a little more tense than usual. I remember thinking at least Old Trafford wasn't all the way over the Pennines, because to be honest I'd often feel a bit sleepy when we played in Yorkshire. I remember arriving at Old Trafford and being quite excited about the whole idea of another final, the challenge was the buzz. It was also against Wigan, who I had quickly grown an extreme dislike for.

In Auckland, I'd grown up with rivalries and had not liked a couple of opposition sides over the years, but this Wigan thing was on a whole new level. I guess in many ways it was driven by the fans and I was quickly drawn into this. They didn't like the pie eaters and I didn't either – in fact when we pulled up in the bus, I recall feeling a real sense of hatred for them. They had beaten us the season before I think, and that was probably another driving motivator, you never forget coming second in the big matches. I was really determined that we would be winners this time and that the Premiership would be Saints'.

The fans in the week leading up to the match were super excited about it and talking with neighbours and people in the street had me pretty hyped. I really loved the passion from the Saints supporters and it's something I'll never forget. I grew up in a house with six brothers and a sister and along with my Mum and Dad there weren't many places you could hide after a match. The critics were everywhere as were the pats on the back when they were deserved, so to come to Saints was like being at home with my family. The truth is something many people shy away from when rugby is concerned. I, however, never minded some straight-up honesty and used this as motivation to try my best from week to week.

I had seen us lose and I had witnessed how the supporters were left disappointed and demoralised. I turned up at Old Trafford and the Saints fans were buoyant, vocal and in large numbers. I recall thinking I just want them to all walk away feeling happy and proud.

I guess the fact that it was a major final, against arch-rival Wigan is quite memorable on its own. The rivalry was intense and any win over them always felt extra rewarding. It was also what I felt was the beginning of the break-up of a side that had played together and had been building towards some clear domination. There was talk that Gaza [Gary Connolly] was being shopped about; for me this was abhorrent to say the least. I recall feeling somewhat let down by a football club who clearly had a different vision to mine. As players the aim is to be the best, to win as often as possible and to make sure the supporters who turn up each week get to see the best.

Gary scored the first try I recall, and it was a super effort. Although he wouldn't put it down as his best try ever, it was one that only someone like him could score.

Coops [Shane Cooper] had kicked it along the ground and Gaza scooped down, collecting it on the way to breaking a deadlock that seemed to last forever, nearly the whole of the first half, I think, without any points. I was pretty elated as were all the fans and the boys. I'm walking back to halfway thinking why the fuck would you sell that kid – it all made no sense and to have thoughts like that running through your mind in a major final, it just seemed insane. I guess on reflection it was a clear example of how incongruence can lead to different paths and it was something that eventually contributed to my departure as well. It wasn't, however, to be our downfall today as the game charged ahead. I recall making a run and Shaun Edwards leg-tripping me; I wanted to drop the ball and go back and give him more than a few whacks around the ears. I was furious and shouted at the ref, who did absolutely nothing. The boys were totally on the game though and nothing was going to stop us today. Lockers was slightly off with the boot, but he did score a lovely try late in the match to make sure we secured the victory. My only regret after the match was that we hadn't given them another good beating like we had given them earlier in the season.

It was a fairly good season as far as match-ups against the arch-rivals go. I recall we had played each other five times that year with two wins each and a draw. They were also gunning for the Grand Slam in the Premiership Final which we were keen to ensure didn't happen. I think we may have also finished level on the points table, with them taking it out on points differential. The overall occasion generated a lot of excitement and expectations which always make these games special. The venue also is of special significance, as it is always nice to play on a pitch and a stadium such as Old Trafford – I personally would prefer Knowsley Road but there were plenty of memorable days there.

That game was the end of the season and as I mentioned above, I felt that it was the beginning of the end for this particular group. As history would reveal, the guys did end up all over the country. I left and guys who I honestly thought would remain one-club men ended up in places I never imagined – Gary at Wigan for a start. It didn't do anything for me apart from bond us as team-mates more than we already were. It also bonded me tighter to the St Helens family, which is something I've always been very proud to have been a part of.

It was a one-off magical moment; having said that we had worked really hard throughout the season and deserved the result that we achieved. I would have to say that my time with Saints definitely taught me all sorts of things that were helpful throughout the rest of my career, character-building traits that made resilience so much easier.

I made a rocky start to my time at Saints and was booed in my first outing where I think I snapped my cruciate again. It only motivated me to try harder, and I didn't want to let the fans down by not performing at my best. I was in a hotel for the first eight weeks that I was there, which was a complete nightmare, almost like self-isolation. I recall reading the newspaper and Murph [Alex Murphy] was quoted in it as saying he wanted me on the next plane out of there. I'm not sure to this day if he did or didn't, but I know that I've always enjoyed the theatrics of the off-the-field performances, especially from legends such as Murph.

I would have loved to have played more under him, as having watched old tapes of him play I always had enormous respect for the great man. He was a real character, as was Mike McClennan, who I was super lucky to have been coached by as well. I recall my first few weeks at Saints when I moved into Chamberlain Street across from Knowsley Road. I woke one morning and walked to the Lippies corner shop to grab a paper and some milk – the walk was only about 100 metres and it took me one hour. I quickly learned that people loved to have a chat and especially about footy. My neighbours here were the best, loved to chat and once again they never held back on the criticism or the praise when deserved. It was a place that I was so happy to be. Saints had come to New Zealand in about 1980 and had played a match at Carlaw Park in Auckland. I was at the match as a young fella and recall thinking I'd love to play for that team one day, I'm not sure that it was because they were so good or whether it was because of the super cool kit they wore. I know one thing for sure now, that it was both that lured me towards what is one of the world's most prestigious rugby clubs.

I have quite a few stories from my time at Saints, but I can't go through them all. Also, I won't name any names either. I could tell you that one of the fastest players in the team was also a pretty fast driver, so fast in fact that he knocked on the front door of a few of my neighbours' homes when dropping me off one night – the problem was it was his car doing the knocking. I could tell you about a cab ride home from Liverpool that ended in the centre of St Helens where everyone getting out was stark naked – someone decided to start ripping shirts and before you knew it no one was clothed ... it was the fastest run I had ever done to home. I could tell you that I was freaked out when I first arrived and a brown paper bag with a bottle of sherry was being passed around, but I won't.

The thing about the guys when I was there was, they had no egos and it was overall a marvellous experience. We would have a beer, train hard and play hard ... living the dream is what I would say.

Coming to the end of my time at Saints, I was becoming somewhat disillusioned with what Saints were doing. I didn't agree with the Gary Connolly business and there were other things going on as well. However, having said that, the chance to head home to Auckland was probably never in doubt. It wasn't anything to do with wanting to play in the Winfield

Cup, I simply wanted to be back in New Zealand where my parents and other family were. If it hadn't been for the Auckland Warriors, I'm not sure where I would have finished my career. I do know that I loved playing with Saints and to this day feel very fortunate to have been given the opportunity.

I went back to the Warriors in Auckland where I played another four seasons before retiring. I had signed to play for Penrith in the 1999 season but I snapped my ACL and that was the last I played. It ended a little as it started, with a torn ACL.

Life is pretty good at the moment. I have five children: Brad was born at Whiston hospital, George, Wendell, Harris and one girl, Romi. They have kept me pretty busy over the years. I also manage a charitable trust that delivers social services to various communities. I have a private practice also where I'm a cognitive behavioural therapist. Having a psychology background has allowed me to give back to communities of need, which is a passion that I continue with today.

I do still follow the Saints a little, I think they are doing really well and enjoy seeing them get great results. I have been back a few times and always love the catch-ups. Facebook these days also makes communicating so much easier, so it's nice to hear from the lads. Janette Smith, the super physio, is like the glue, like our mum (even if some of us are older) who communicates and keeps us all together. One big extended family.

DAVE FAIRLEIGH

Dave Fairleigh

PROP/SECOND ROW 2001
HERITAGE NUMBER 1102

BORN: 1 September 1970, Wyoming, New South Wales

SIGNED: 2001 from Newcastle Knights

DEBUT: 26 January 2001 vs Brisbane Broncos

LAST GAME: 6 October 2001 vs Wigan Warriors

ST HELENS CAREER: 32 appearances (including one as a substitute), 8 tries

HONOURS: World Club Challenge 2001; Challenge Cup Final 2001

LEFT: 2002 Retired

PLAYING CAREER: North Sydney Bears (1989–99), Newcastle Knights (2000), St Helens (2001)

Dave Fairleigh may have only played one season for the Saints in Super League, but not one supporter will have a bad word to say about the big man – I think every single fan who remembers him will wish he had stayed longer.

The Australian joined St Helens from Newcastle Knights. He had previously spent a decade at the North Sydney Bears and only left after they merged with Manly Sea Eagles to become the Northern Eagles.

He only spent one season with the Knights and was named the club's Player of the Year, Players' Player of the Year and the Coaches' Player of the Year. He then decided it was time to try his hand in England and he instantly fell in love in with St Helens, and that love was more than reciprocated.

Fairleigh was a no-nonsense forward and never backed down from a challenge. The record books state that he won the World Club Challenge and Challenge Cup in his one and only season, but the legacy he left at the club is massive and will live on for ever.

During this chapter, it is obvious that Fairleigh enjoyed his time at Saints and he reveals that it is his dream to one day become head coach of St Helens Rugby League Football Club.

St Helens 22-8 Wigan Warriors
Challenge Cup Fourth Round
Saturday, 10 February 2001
Knowsley Road, St Helens
Attendance 13,593

Teams

St Helens	*Wigan Warriors*
Paul Wellens	Kris Radlinski
Sean Hoppe	Brett Dallas
Kevin Iro	Steve Renouf
Paul Newlove	Gary Connolly
Anthony Sullivan	Paul Johnson
Tommy Martyn	Matty Johns
Sean Long	Adrian Lam
Dave Fairleigh	Terry O'Connor
Keiron Cunningham	Terry Newton
Sonny Nickle	Neil Cowie
Chris Joynt	Dave Furner
Peter Shiels	Denis Betts
Paul Sculthorpe	Andy Farrell

Subs

Tony Stewart	Mick Cassidy
Steve Hall	Simon Haughton
Tim Jonkers	Wes Davies
John Stankevich	Harvey Howard

Coaches

Ian Millward	Frank Endacott

Tries

Sullivan	Connolly
Joynt	
Jonkers	
Stewart	

Goals

Long (3)	Farrell (2)

Referee: Stuart Cummings

Some people frown when you choose a player that has not played that many games, but this chapter with Dave Fairleigh is a must-read for any Saints fan.

The game Fairleigh has chosen was only his third game for the club. He played in a friendly against Salford and then in the World Club Challenge against Brisbane Broncos, but it was his next game that stands out more than others.

Super League clubs entered the Challenge Cup in the fourth round and Saints and Wigan had been drawn against each other at Knowsley Road. For people born in both towns, this is the game they want to see every week, but sometimes the occasion gets too big for so-called outsiders.

In this chapter, Fairleigh reveals that it didn't take him too long to realise what this game meant to everyone. He still has the battle wounds to prove it.

He goes into detail about how Wigan were determined to rough him up and put him off his game, and it was after breaking his nose in that match that he realised he needed to step up and be counted. And from that moment on, he promised never to take a backward step against anyone from Wigan.

This chapter also reveals the reason he left the club after just one season despite having agreed a new contract, while Fairleigh also goes into detail about the reason he left a well-paid job as assistant coach at the North Queensland Cowboys and what he is up to now.

I came to St Helens and I was probably their major signing for the new season. I'd heard about the rivalry between St Helens and Wigan and people were telling me that Wigan and Saints just hate each other and things like that, so I sort of heard about it but I didn't really think too much of it.

There are rivalries in the NRL and things like that, so it didn't really bother me.

We beat Brisbane Broncos in the World Club Challenge and then the Challenge Cup draw was made and the two heavyweights of Saints and Wigan came out together in round one [it was the fourth round, but it was the first round that Super League clubs had been involved in], and I obviously had an idea of how big the Challenge Cup was because as a kid I used to wake up in the early hours in Australia and watch it on TV.

We used to love the Challenge Cup, we always made sure we watched the English football [rugby league] in our family.

So, it was Saints versus Wigan in the Challenge Cup at Knowsley Road, I was their major signing and I remember walking to the ground and warming up, you could really feel the atmosphere building. I knew Wigan were a good side, they had some good players led by Andrew Farrell and Terry O'Connor, I think Steve Renouf and Dave Furner were two of the Aussies they had signed at the time. We ran out and it was just electric, it was unbelievable. I've had that feeling before in other games, how the crowd are into it and it's a big game; you knew it was a big game because Saints were the reigning champions and Wigan have always been a great team.

About three minutes into the game, I was absolutely getting smashed from pillar to post. They were into me; I had already had stitches and I think my nose was broken. Whatever foul play they could get away with, they did it to me. They were out to send a real message that said, this is English football – rugby league. I just remember distinctly at the time, I was checking myself and I thought, 'Fuck, I've got to fucking aim up here.' This was like a moment that they were either going to put it over me or I'm going to stand up and take them on. So, I just totally changed my mindset. I guess I got caught up in the side show that was a Saints v Wigan derby and didn't understand the seriousness of it and how big it really is. Having not truly given it the respect it deserved I found out after about 20 minutes and I made the decision to totally change my attitude. After that, I just ripped in and gave it back as good as I got, and I was determined not to let anyone get the better of me.

It was my first Challenge Cup game for St Helens and we were at Knowsley Road and I really wanted to put on a good showing and make sure it was one I was happy with and also a performance the club and the fans would be happy with. The game went on and it was a really good, close game. I gave back as good as I got. Someone had mentioned to me when I signed for the club that Saints always win close games, they always seem to win late. I just remember thinking, that's good. Again, not really giving it too much attention, because the players never really spoke about things like that. In that season, the number of games we came from behind and won late was amazing. I learned by the end of the year that mentally we had things covered. If it was a close game with five or ten minutes left on the clock, I think teams just knew that we were going to win. I can remember we scored two late tries and kicked the goal and we won the game near the end, I can remember thinking wow, this is just everything that everyone has told me about St Helens. And it all happened in my first game – well, my first proper game against an English opponent.

They absolutely gave it to me, so I had to step up to the plate big time. The crowd were unreal, and by the end of the game they were chanting my name. I'm thinking wow, this is just unbelievable. We had just knocked Wigan out of the Challenge Cup, so I was like, 'Righto, this is game-on here.' I was loving it. It was exactly what I signed up for. I think we ended up playing Wigan six times that year – it was four times through the regular season, once in the Challenge Cup and then once in the Super League play-off semi-finals. I made a promise to myself that I was never going to let anyone from Wigan put it over me again. I think the next time we met was the Good Friday game and to be honest, I can't remember if we won or lost but it was a close game, but I remember me and Andy Farrell were just going at it hammer and tongs for the whole game. Physically and verbally. I have a lot of respect for Andy Farrell because he was a great player, but I was at him, saying, 'Mate, you've never proved yourself in the NRL. You've got to go over there Andy, you're a nobody.' He was giving it as good as he could as well, I just remember that I made that promise to myself that I was never going to let anyone from Wigan get the better of me or play bad against Wigan, because I knew how much it meant to the club and the fans. I actually got man of the match that day from Sky Sports. So, my first few encounters with Wigan really stick out in my mind.

There are a number of other games that live fondly in the memory – the Challenge Cup Final being one of them. I guess the biggest disappointment during that year – remember we had such a fantastic team in 2001 – Sean Long did his ACL about six games out from the play-offs. When you lose a player of his calibre – half-back, kicking game – he had everything, to readjust and go on and try and win the competition is a big ask. Whilst we still believed we could do it, we headed over to the JJB Stadium to face Wigan and we knew that if we won that we would go to the Grand Final at Old Trafford. We did everything possible and gave it a good go, but we just had nothing left. Longy was like our little general, he would direct us around the park and would come up with the big plays when we needed them. He was a massive competitor, but with him injured we didn't have that and when you lose your number seven like that it makes it extremely difficult. We just didn't have enough to get across the line, but we would have won the comp if Longy had been fit, I'm so confident about that.

My time at St Helens was amazing. It may have only been a year, but even now nearly 20 years later I still have friends there. The fondest memory of St Helens for me is that my daughter was born there. I'll always have a connection with the town, I was really proud to go to that club because as a kid I used to watch when Mal [Meninga] played there and all the great names that represented the club, right down to Alex Murphy. It was such a shame that my father had passed away, so he never got to see that but I just know that would have been probably the proudest moment for him of my whole career, in me joining St Helens.

I went there, I had a number of good offers from teams in Australia, but I thought, 'You know what, let's do it.' It was almost like closing my eyes, holding my breath and just signing the contract, just see how it goes and where this adventure takes us. I can honestly say it is one of the greatest things I ever did. When I agreed the move, it was initially just for one season, because I wanted to know if I would like it in England. I was 31 years of age, so if I was playing in today's game I would have probably played until I was 34 but I was sort of at the crossover of eras – half old school and half the science of the game coming in. I think the early parts of my career, the way they trained and recovered and things like that, regarding the science, there was none at all. I paid the price for that in the back-end of my career. Having said that, I was really enjoying my time at St Helens, so the club said did I want to stay on, and I actually agreed and I signed for another year. It was a good contract.

I had signed on before the first season had finished and the semis had started. I was sitting in the sheds before we went out on the field to warm up. I knew my role, I knew what I had to do and if I did it, I would play well. I had really set the bar high and I had high expectations of what I did and took pride in what I delivered for the football club. I was never a person who would just take the money and run, I feel like I have to give my all. I was watching Wello [Paul Wellens], Longy and a couple of others there and they were just dancing around and high fiving each other, all pumped up ready to play. I was just sitting there thinking we are warming up in five, looking at my watch. I just looked at the spark and the energy that those players had, don't get me wrong I had that, but it was internal and I was just sitting there because I was like ten years older than these blokes. I had been in their shoes and I had walked their path and I just thought it might be time to finish. I also had an underlying shoulder problem and I knew it needed surgery. I thought, 'I can't do this anymore.' It wouldn't be right to do it to the club because if I did, I can honestly say I don't think I would have been able to produce what I had done that year again. It took so much out of me because I was just so committed to the team and to every session, I wanted to be the first at training and the last to leave. I wanted to set an example to all the young blokes.

We had some good youngsters coming through with the likes of Paul Sculthorpe and I wanted to be an example for them on how to be a professional. I wanted to pass on my experience to them and help them, but I made that decision there in that dressing shed that I couldn't honestly look the club in the eye and say 'I am going to give you as good as I did this year' and take their money. So, I told Eamon [McManus]. He was obviously disappointed, but he respected the fact that I told him in my heart that I would just be taking the money if I stayed. Yes, I would have played, and I probably would have played some good games but it was the fact that I couldn't consistently do it, I didn't think I had it in me to play on a consistent level for a whole season at the level that I would deem acceptable for myself. Not anyone else, but for myself. People would always come up and say, 'Yeah Dave, you had a great game, well done,' but you know deep down if you had a good game or not. Whether you win or you lose, it's a horrible feeling when people say you had a great game but you know you didn't. You can kind of hide in a team environment, but I don't like that feeling. If someone says I've had a good game, I want to know deep down that I have had a good game. I just didn't have that anymore. I had some injuries and surgeries, but I had just come to a stage that it wouldn't be honest to take the money from St Helens and not deliver.

Going back to that Wigan game, I don't think I could have asked for a better game to help me get used to playing footy in England. The way we trained and how hard we trained leading up to that game really gave me a shock. I didn't expect the training to be like the NRL, but I can honestly say I don't think I trained as hard as I did at St Helens at any other club. I thought, 'Wow, this is not a two-bob operation, these guys mean business.' I watched my new team-mates and you could see how hungry and talented they were. I was very conscious not to come over and be the Aussie and tell them how much better the NRL is over Super League. I had to fit in, and I learned very quickly that I had to fit in with them. I didn't want to be one of those guys constantly saying, 'Well, back home we do it like this.' You do it the St Helens way. So, I worked out really quickly that I had to fit in with them. That Challenge Cup tie early on absolutely mentally prepared me for the games that were coming up. Particularly against

Bradford; we played them a number of times and I knew I always played well against Bradford. It was the lesser teams that were harder for me. I wouldn't say I didn't enjoy playing teams like that – I would rather play a tough, close game than a game where you turn up to the ground and you know you are going to win.

When you played Wigan or Bradford at that time, or Leeds, you didn't know whether you were going to win or not. You know all you can do is the best you can, if everyone does their job, we execute and we hang on to the football, we will win the game. There were teams there at that time and no disrespect to anyone, but you knew we would win. We are St Helens; we might make some errors but we know we will win this game.

There is a huge focus on defence in Australian rugby league. There is an attacking element, but teams are very heavily geared defensively, so we [Saints] had won a number of games and we had won some close ones. I'm going to digress a little bit now, so bear with me.

I actually used the video 'Wide to West' in a presentation I gave recently about having a positive mindset. I told them I had been involved in a team that had this positive mindset and this belief that they could win no matter what the circumstances were and no matter how bad the situation was. It was just there, the funny thing was nobody actually ever said it, we never spoke about it or it didn't have a name or anything like that. It didn't have anything, it was just there and that's why I use the 'Wide to West' video: that's it, that's the mindset. It was the year before I joined, but that's what St Helens could produce when we needed to.

Sorry for digressing, I'll get back to my point. I didn't like that feeling of turning up knowing we were going to win. I didn't like that feeling at all because you don't have that mental edge, that toughness and relentless edge that you need to win a game of football. Well, you do have it, but you have got to dig really, really deep to find it. It's very easy to play footy against crap teams. I prided myself on playing well against good teams, making sure I did my job against the good teams. I know I did that.

I wish I had gone to St Helens earlier. I wish I had had three or four years there. I'm good friends with Matt Gidley, Peter Shiels and Jamie Lyon and I know Mal well, along with Darren Britt – all who played for Saints at some point. St Helens don't just sign anyone, there is a genuine expectation that you have to deliver when you play for St Helens because of the name and the history of the club and the people that have worn that jersey. You definitely feel it, I know I felt it. I remember in the pre-season, every time I looked up, whether it was weights or running, Paul Sculthorpe would be looking at me. If I was running and I was winning, Sculthorpe would be behind me and he'd try and beat me, then I'd push back and try and get over him. He probably had seven or eight years on me, but he brought the best out of me. The likes of Keiron [Cunningham], Scully and all the big names, I could just feel them all looking at me. They were looking at me thinking, what is this guy like? Is he going to be just another Aussie that comes over here and takes the cash and tells everyone how good the NRL is and how shit the Super League is?

The first thing for me that was important, was that I got the respect of the players and the team. The only way to get that is obviously at training. You need to train the best you can and then deliver on the field. Once I knew I had the respect of the team, it was just a great feeling knowing that your team-mates look at you and they know you are not going to let them down. One thing I can say about my time at St Helens in the games that I played in, not once did I ever dog it, not once did I ever put in a half-rated effort. I can honestly say I gave everything I had in every game for St Helens.

Since leaving Saints, I have been assistant coach at a number of clubs and I was really disappointed with my manager because Rushy [Saints chief executive Mike Rush] had come out to Australia, this was when they were signing Kristian Woolf as coach, and I didn't even know about it. I said to my manager, 'Mate, that's my dream job.' He just said, 'Oh, I thought you were happy where you are.' I could have cried, honestly. I couldn't believe it. I was at North Queensland Cowboys as an assistant coach, I was coaching the likes of Jonathan Thurston and it was a great job. But to get the opportunity to coach St Helens is still a goal of mine, I absolutely want to do that.

I resigned as assistant coach because I didn't believe in the way the Cowboys were being coached and my philosophies on coaching were not in line with the head coach's ones. I had two years left on my contract, again it's very similar to the reason I left St Helens. I honestly thought to myself, 'I can't be here.' Rugby league is a tough game and relentless and it's too hard not to enjoy. My life philosophies and how I believe you treat people and what your style of play is in attack and defence were now in direct contrast to what the head coach's were; it wasn't going to help anyone and I wasn't going to contribute to the team. I could sit there and coach the likes of Michael Morgan and take credit for their games as assistant coach, but my heart just wasn't in it, so I just walked away. There was a role available with the referees. Currently the NRL has 22 full-time referees, they really need them to be a team and be united and have high standards. So, they had a job there and I was reading the description and it just sounded really interesting. I'm still coaching, you are still getting the best out of a person and a team, as there are 22 of them. You analyse their performances, why they are doing things a certain way, what would happen if you did it this way, but it's with the refs.

My team are the referees. I have never engaged more with a group of people on many fronts – individually, collectively or as a group, in so many different ways – than I have by working with the referees. I walked away from North Queensland and took a job for half the money I was on, but I am enjoying it more. It is actually making me a better coach. I have no doubt about that. The role is a bit different to what some previous coaches have done. Michael Maguire spent a year doing it, Ivan Cleary spent a bit of time doing it. The NRL has created this role because they saw a need for the referees to be much more united, have a better understanding about professionalism and leadership. It's all about the team and not about them. I'm really enjoying it; I'd enjoy coaching St Helens more but at this point in time it's a nice little break and breather from the grind of the NRL. I feel good about the fact that I walked away on my terms knowing that I didn't believe in what was happening, so I wasn't just going to stay there.

My first year in first grade was my first year out of high school. I was 18. It was really prestigious to make the Australian schoolboys' team, which I did, then I was under contract with the North Sydney Bears. I played a few games in the lower grade and then got elevated to the first-grade team. I was looking at players that only two years previous I was collecting on footy cards, but one of my first games for the Bears was against Balmain Tigers and I was only 18. The game was at the North Sydney Oval and their pack was Steve Roach (Australia), Ben Ellias (Australia), they had a guy called

Steve Edmed who was a solid front-rower, they had second-rower Bruce McGuire (Australia), Paul Sironen (Australia) and Wayne Pearce (Australia). And here is Dave Fairleigh, one year out of high school ready to take the kick-off. I remember Blocker [Roach] just gave it to me, he didn't stop. They wanted to test the new kid out and they made sure they did that. I got tested out alright.

Where does Dazey come from? I think because I was so in awe of who I was with and playing in the NRL, there was probably about a month where the coach would say, 'Mate, are you listening? You are always in a daze. Every time I say something, I have to say "Dave, what did I say?" You are always in a daze.' And I was. They were calling these plays and I'm like, 'I've never heard that before, what's that?' So, I was constantly in a daze. I remember my first year in first grade, we had City v Country rep games and I made the City rep team. You are talking about players like Michael O'Connor, Andrew Ettingshausen, Benny Ellias, Steve Roach – legends of the game. We were in a training session and I could always tackle, I was a good defender. It was our first training session and the great Jack Gibson was the coach, and Andrew Ettingshausen went up to Jack and I was right next to him and ET said, 'Jack, are we using up-and-in defence or slide defence?' I didn't know what either of them were and Jack goes, 'ET, you can use fucking shit defence for all I care, just tackle them.' I thought, 'That's good, I know that, I can do that.' I was just a kid thrown into the first grade, it was basically 'get in there and swim like hell'.

The game has changed a lot, it's good now with the science and the welfare and all the things they do for the young kids coming through, but back then it was just 'get in, do your best and learn the hard way' and I did. That's where Dazey comes from. People automatically think Daisy the flower, which I get, but the people that know me well when they send me an email or something, they always put D A Z E Y, so that's a true story.

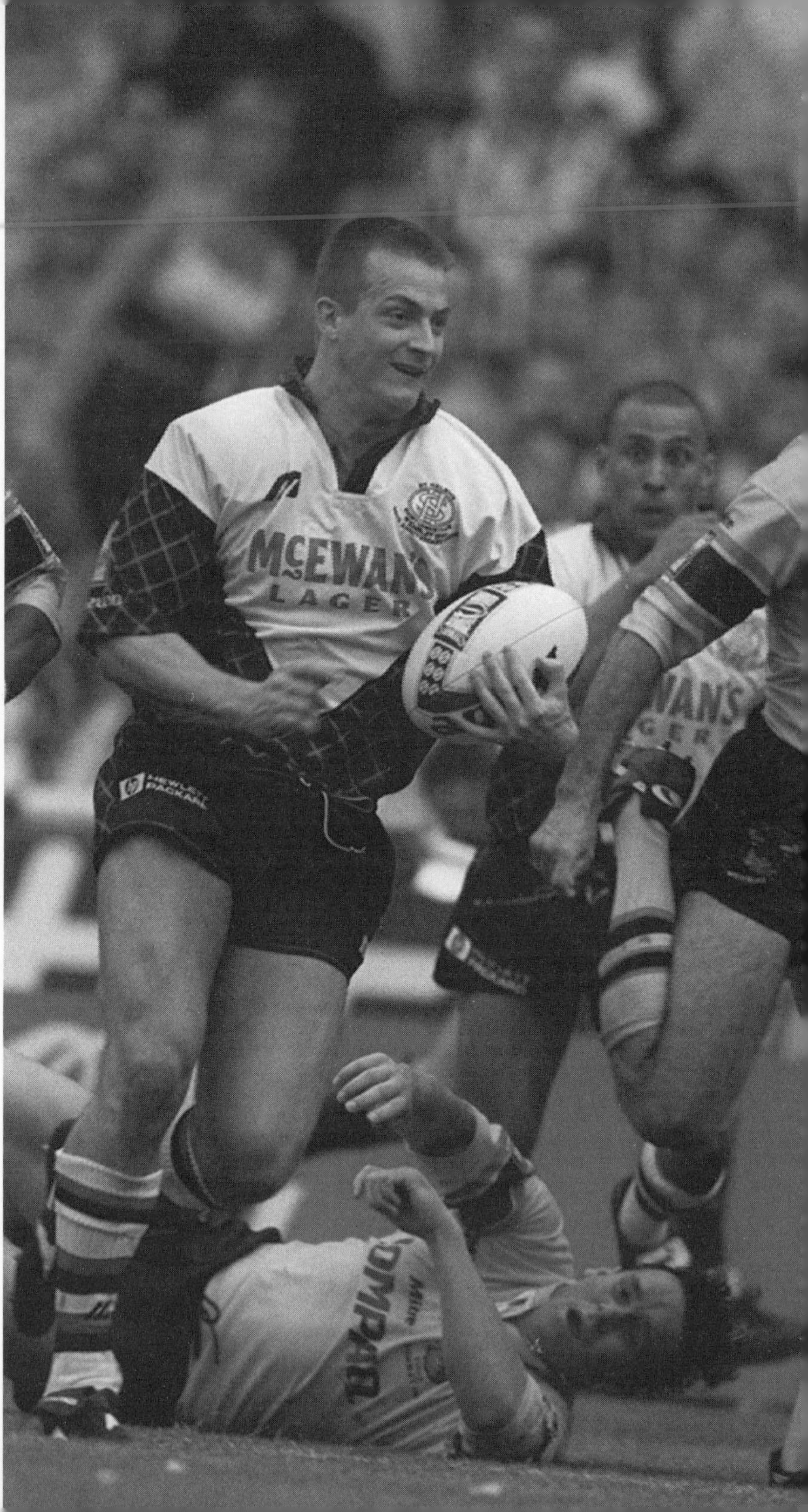

PAUL NEWLOVE

Paul Newlove

CENTRE 1995–2003
HERITAGE NUMBER 1064

BORN: 10 August 1971, Pontefract, England

SIGNED: 29 November 1995 from Bradford Northern

DEBUT: 3 December 1995 vs Wigan Warriors

LAST GAME: 3 October 2003 vs Wigan Warriors

ST HELENS CAREER: 208 appearances, 134 tries

HONOURS: Challenge Cup 1996, 1997, 2001; Super League 1996, 1999, 2002; World Club Challenge 2001; League Leaders' Shield 2002

PLAYING CAREER: Featherstone Rovers (1988–93), Bradford Northern (1993–95), St Helens (1995–2003), Castleford Tigers 2004.

Paul Newlove is a bona-fide rugby league legend. Not just at St Helens, but in the game as a whole. Some people might argue he was not the most hard-working player ever to lace a pair of boots, but none of those people actually shared a dressing room, training field or pitch with him.

He joined St Helens for a world record fee of around £500,000 – which consisted of £250,000 in cash and three players in Sonny Nickle, Bernard Dwyer and Paul Loughlin – as he moved to Saints from Bradford Northern.

That was a lot of money in those days, but St Helens certainly got their worth out of him as he scored 134 tries in 208 appearances for the club, as he helped them win three Super League titles, three Challenge Cups and one World Club Challenge.

Newlove was part of the era that saw St Helens become the most dominant team in England. They took to the newly formed Super League like ducks to water, as they soon became the team to beat as they finally took the mantle of the number one club side in England from their fierce rivals Wigan Warriors.

Newlove will go down as one of the greatest centres to ever play in the modern era, and international fans will always remember the part he played in England's run to the 1995 World Cup Final. He scored four tries altogether in that competition – including one in the final – as they were beaten by Australia 16-8 at Wembley Stadium.

St Helens 20-18 Brisbane Broncos
World Club Challenge
Friday, 26 January 2001
Reebok Stadium, Bolton. Attendance 16,041

Teams

St Helens	*Brisbane Broncos*
Paul Wellens	Darren Lockyer
Sean Hoppe	Lote Tuqiri
Kevin Iro	Stuart Kelly
Paul Newlove	Michael De Vere
Anthony Sullivan	Wendell Sailor
Tommy Martyn	Shaun Berrigan
Sean Long	Scott Prince
Dave Fairleigh	Shane Webcke
Keiron Cunningham	Luke Priddis
Sonny Nickle	Petero Civoniceva
Chris Joynt	Gorden Tallis
Peter Shiels	Dane Carlaw
Paul Sculthorpe	Philip Lee

Subs

Tim Jonkers	Shane Walker
Vila Matautia	Ashley Harrison
John Stankevitch	Brad Meyers
Anthony Stewart	Chris Walker

Coaches

Ian Millward	Wayne Bennett

Tries

Joynt	Berrigan
Long	Lee
Sculthorpe	Meyers

Goals

Long (3)	De Vere (3)

Drop Goals
Long
Sculthorpe

Referee: Stuart Cummings

When you have played more than 200 games for one club and won every single trophy on offer, it is quite difficult to pick out just one game that stands above the rest.

After taking a while to think about it, Newlove decided to choose a game that was more of a team performance than an individual one as St Helens defeated NRL champions Brisbane Broncos in the 2001 World Club Challenge.

Newlove goes into detail about how they prepared and how he felt this game was being taken more seriously than previous World Club Challenges. He believed everything was put in place for them to be successful and that this was not going to be treated as a friendly encounter.

Saints defended like their lives depended on it in this game and Newlove remembers the moment he knew they would beat the Broncos – and all thanks had to go to the good old British weather.

Newlove also explains the reason he left Bradford to join St Helens, and why Peter Fox once again played a prominent role in his career.

Also in this chapter, Newlove reveals how he was hurt that he didn't get the chance to have a testimonial year at Saints, but insists that time is a great healer and everything is water under the bridge now.

There are a lot of games I could actually choose from my eight years at St Helens, but there is one that really sticks out in my mind. I wouldn't actually say it was my best game personally, I'm talking about the team as a whole, and that game was against Brisbane Broncos at Bolton Wanderers' football ground in the World Club Challenge.

It was the first WCC one in 2001. (He was part of the team that lost in 2003.) I think there were only two points in it and we just nicked it at the end. It was a really hard-fought game, was that one. The build-up to the game was quite special. We went over to Lanzarote and we had a week over there prior to the game. We went to a place called Club la Santa and it was really, really good.

The facilities and the field we used were spectacular. It was nice to train in those warm conditions, you must remember it was at the end of January when we were playing and the weather in England wasn't up to scratch. So, to train in the sun out there was nice. That week, we trained the house down. It was great, we were training on the field and everyone was together, so it was good. The feeling among the group was great.

Ian Millward was the coach at the time, and you could see that Millward wanted to win this trophy. He wasn't messing about; this meant a lot to him and he wanted to win. We were playing to win this World Club Challenge, I say this because some World Club Challenges – I'm not mentioning any coaches – but some that we have played in, they have never really been taken that serious and basically they treated the World Club Challenge as a warm-up game. This year,

Ian Millward wanted to win and put the gauntlet down. Training out there was good, and the intensity was high, I think it did us the world of good. When you go away like that, you know you are doing it for a purpose as well, there is something at the end of it. It was a special time. That was the first World Club Challenge that we all played in and it was a high-intensity game against a tough Australian team.

The build-up for that game was really, really good. It was a cold night in Bolton, it was toe-to-toe all the way through the game and there wasn't much in it. In the second half, I sidestepped Brisbane's Australian international winger Wendell Sailor and made a break down the left-hand side. I then drew the full-back and put the ball back inside to Joynty [Chris Joynt] and Joynty went over and scored a try. The heavens then opened, and the rain came down and it was like a blizzard. Hailstones were coming down and everything. All the Brisbane players weren't expecting the conditions they got, they are used to playing in the warm sunshine in Brisbane and Australia and they were stood behind the sticks shivering and wondering what was going on.

Once we scored that try, we went on to win the game. It was close but our defence that night from 1 to 13 plus the subs – everyone involved – was outstanding. Everyone defended like their life depended on it. Like I say, it was a really, really good team effort. When the snow and hailstones came down, that helped us a lot and it's a memory I will always take from that game. I think that game set a marker for the club and Super League.

When I joined St Helens, we were THE team to beat. We won the Challenge Cup and Super League in my first season in 1996. We were winning major trophies, so during that era we were the team in Super League that everyone wanted to beat. To then beat Brisbane in 2001, it was a big scalp for the club and for us as players. It was massive for the English Super League as well.

How did my move to St Helens come about? Well, Peter Fox was in charge of Bradford at the time, the club were not going to renew Peter's contract at Bradford and I got an inkling that he was going to leave and they were actually already looking for a new coach. I had the utmost respect for Peter. I actually only went to Bradford because Peter was the coach. I went up to him and said, 'I don't want to stay here if you are not going to be here, Peter.'

Peter was my coach at Featherstone Rovers, and he knew my game and I honestly didn't want to be at the club without him. That's how talk of a move came about, Saints must have got wind of it. I actually think Peter rang Eric Ashton at Saints and Eric took it to the board and asked if they were interested. They had recently lost Gary Connolly to Wigan, so they were looking for a new centre and the timing was perfect to be honest. It just went from there really. Saints had a board meeting and they said, 'Yeah, we'll try and sign him.' That got the ball rolling and I signed for Saints, everything went through and I become a St Helens player. I played the last few games of the 1995/96 campaign, but my first season at Saints was the first ever Super League season. It was great to win those trophies in my first year at Saints. At the end of the day, that is the reason I signed for St Helens. It was to win trophies, it's as simple as that.

Up until then, they were always the second team behind Wigan, were St Helens, so I was made up to go to St Helens. To play in a great team, I could add my little bit to the team and play with players like Chris Joynt, Paul Wellens, Anthony Sullivan, Tommy Martyn – the list goes on really. It was a dream come true for me; it really was. I have always played in teams that never really kicked on. I started at Featherstone Rovers. I enjoyed my time at Featherstone, but I was not playing with great players. Don't get me wrong, they were good players for that particular team, but if I wanted to improve, I needed to move on and play with better players. Eventually I did that and ended up playing week in, week out with the likes of Bobbie Goulding as he was there then. So, it was great to go to St Helens and play in a team littered with stars.

I really enjoyed my time at St Helens, I actually wish I could have had a testimonial there, I really do. I did eight years at Saints, before they got rid of me. Ian Millward was still the coach at that time. I had snapped my Achilles but I actually came back after that and the year after that injury I was the top try scorer in Super League. Millward said to me, 'You are my best centre this year.' He had a meeting with me and told me I was his best centre and that I was playing well. After hearing that, I'm thinking 'great'. That was the last year of my contract, my deal ran out at the end of that year and I thought, 'As long as I keep doing well, I might get an extension on my contract.' I just wanted two more years, so I could get my testimonial at Saints. I really wanted to do 10 years at the club.

They then went and signed a Samoan utility player from Australia in Willie Talau. He could play anywhere in the backs, but I think they got him to replace me and Ian said to me, 'Don't worry, he's just a utility player. We'll use him everywhere.' Which they did, he did play a bit of everywhere, and then they told me they were not going to renew my contract. That was the end of it, and I knew then that Willie Talau was going to fill my position at centre once I'd left. It is business, it's only the same thing as when Paul Loughlin left – he was a legend at St Helens – I'm sure he felt the same when they signed me because he was in the deal along with Bernard Dwyer and Sonny Nickle to go to Bradford.

At the end of the day, it happens to everybody, even the best players. You have to come to an end at some point, and if the club can make money off you or they have a younger player coming through, they will do it. At the time, I was 31 or 32, so I was coming to the back-end of my career, so it is business but at the time it was a hard pill to swallow. Especially when you have done your best for the club and helped them win trophies, and being a big part of that success with the tries I scored and things like that. It is a bitter pill to swallow, but now it's all over and it's all forgotten about.

It was definitely the best time of my career without any doubt, those years at St Helens. I enjoyed my time at Featherstone, I did five years there. I started out there and they are my local side. I have history with the club, my dad was captain there and played at Wembley himself, my brother played there as well, so Featherstone is my local team round where I live in Pontefract. I then moved to Bradford, but St Helens is the club that I would like to think I'm more well known for in the rugby league world.

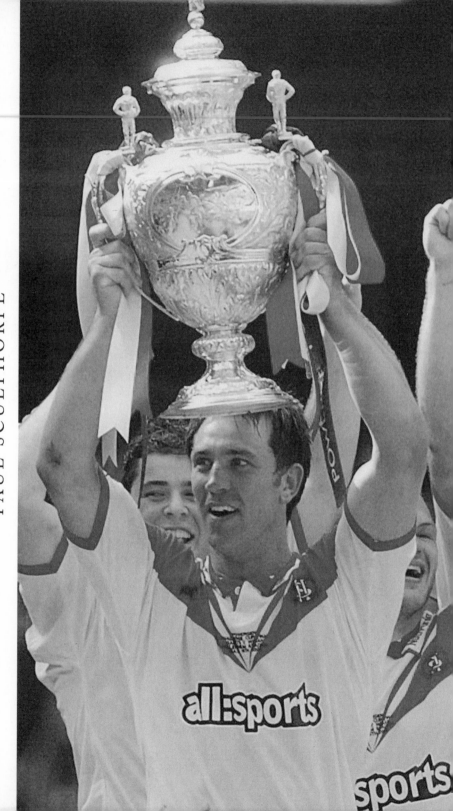

PAUL SCULTHORPE

Paul Sculthorpe

LOOSE FORWARD/SECOND ROW 1998–2008
HERITAGE NUMBER 1083

BORN: 22 September 1977, Burnley, England

SIGNED: 1 January 1998 from Warrington Wolves

DEBUT: 15 February 1998 vs Featherstone Rovers

LAST GAME: 30 August 2008 v Hull FC

ST HELENS CAREER: 261 appearances (including 5 as a substitute), 113 tries, 392 goals, 10 drop goals

HONOURS: Challenge Cup 2001, 2004, 2006, 2008; Super League 1999, 2000, 2002; World Club Challenge 2001, 2007; League Leaders' Shield 2002, 2005, 2006, 2007; Man of Steel 2001, 2002

PLAYING CAREER: Warrington Wolves (1996–97), St Helens (1998–2008)

When you think of St Helens RLFC, one of the first players you think of is Paul Sculthorpe. 'Scully' is one of the biggest names in the sport – even today – and his ten years at the club saw him win three Super League titles, four Challenge Cups, four League Leaders' Shields, two World Club Challenges and he is still the only player to have won back-to-back Man of Steel awards.

When St Helens signed Scully from Warrington Wolves for a fee of £375,000 – a record transfer fee for a forward – a lot of people raised their eyebrows and said that it was too much of a gamble. It is safe to say that it was money well spent.

Scully was the ultimate professional, playing the game with his heart on his sleeve. You don't have to be a Saints fan to have been an admirer of his career. His performances alone for Great Britain against Australia will always see him as one of the legends of the game.

His love for St Helens is clear for all to see, even to this day. He still spends a lot of time at the club and is always willing to donate his time to the club in any way he can. Paul Sculthorpe is not only one of the best players to ever play for St Helens, he is up there with the likes of Ellery Hanley, Billy Boston and Alex Murphy as one of the best players to ever play the game.

St Helens 32-16 Wigan Warriors

Challenge Cup Final
Saturday, 15 May 2004
Millennium Stadium, Cardiff
Attendance 73,734

Teams

St Helens	*Wigan Warriors*
Paul Wellens	Kris Radlinski
Ade Gardner	David Hodgson
Martin Gleeson	Sean O'Loughlin
Willie Talau	Kevin Brown
Darren Albert	Brett Dallas
Jason Hooper	Danny Orr
Sean Long	Adrian Lam
Nick Fozzard	Quentin Pongia
Keiron Cunningham	Terry Newton
Keith Mason	Craig Smith
Chris Joynt	Danny Tickle
Lee Gilmour	Gareth Hock
Paul Sculthorpe	Andy Farrell

Subs

Dominic Feaunati	Stephen Wild
Jon Wilkin	Mick Cassidy
Ricky Bibey	Danny Sculthorpe
Mark Edmondson	Terry O'Connor

Coaches

Ian Millward	Mike Gregory

Tries

Gilmour	Newton
Talau (2)	Dallas (2)
Wellens	
Sculthorpe	

Goals

Long (6)	Farrell (2)

Referee: Karl Kirkpatrick

Scully's selected game has already been mentioned in this book, but everyone has their own memories and this one stands out in his mind for two special reasons – it was his first trophy as Saints captain and the whole day was a special family affair.

Scully writes about how the day was turned into a brother versus brother event, with Danny lining up against him in the Wigan team. Paul also reveals that out of all the stadiums he has played in throughout his career, the Millennium Stadium in Cardiff is his favourite.

Rugby league die-hards will enjoy his remarks about Twickenham – his comments in this chapter are based on the atmosphere and what he personally gets out of a stadium. It is not a league versus union jibe.

Scully goes into detail about that famous incident at Knowsley Road on Good Friday when a bust-up happened deep in Wigan's half, and Scully as captain of Saints squared up to Wigan skipper Andy Farrell. There was a lot of pushing and shoving and a few obscenities thrown, it was pure theatre, and everyone loved it. A lot of fans would love to read about a deep hatred between Scully and Faz and that this incident was because of bad blood over the years – sorry to disappoint. Scully admits this was just in the heat of the battle and they are very good friends away from the game and have been since they were kids.

The game that probably stands out the most for me is the one I always speak about when I talk at dinners and things like that. It's probably not necessarily my best game individually or anything like that, but the one that stands out is the 2004 Challenge Cup Final against Wigan in Cardiff.

That was my first final as captain of Saints and obviously to beat Wigan at what was, for me, the best ground I have ever played at atmosphere-wise, the Millennium Stadium, made it a special day. And to make the event more special, my brother was on the opposite side to me that day.

A lot of the attention in the build-up to that game was on Danny and myself, I think we were the first brothers in over 60 years to play against each other in a Challenge Cup Final. So, a lot of the build-up was focused on us. Clare Balding and some of the BBC crew were round at my parents' house and we did a lot of interviews that week with us playing against each other. So yeah, it was a pretty full-on week.

I remember we stopped at the Vale of Glamorgan – which is the Wales Rugby Union base – and we stayed there a few days before the final. Everything just went to plan, I can honestly say that. It was a great build-up. I remember quite a bit about the game; we got off to a flying start. We were just on it straight from the off, I think Jason Hooper chased down Kris Radlinski's kick and Willie Talau picked it up and Lee Gilmour scored so it was a pretty quick start and we just really hit them from the off.

We were in control all the way through. Wigan had a great side in 2004 and they did come back at us a few times but I think we were always in control of that game and never in any danger of losing. I scored a pretty important try as well that day that gave us a bit of breathing space, so yeah, it was great.

I always speak about when I was growing up as a kid and watching the Challenge Cup Final on the TV and watching the captains walk up those steps and lift the trophy and I got the opportunity to do just that. It didn't take any gloss off for me that it wasn't played at Wembley, not at all. We'd played at Wembley before and we had played a few away from Wembley as well.

We played at Twickenham in 2001, which was probably one of the worst games I have been involved with. It was brilliant in regards that we had won it and it was a great performance, but it was just disappointing. Twickenham was shite. The weather was awful as well, it was just everything. It wasn't good apart from us absolutely smashing Bradford. I think Twickenham is lifeless, but the Millennium Stadium was brilliant. It is quite high, and everyone is right on top of you, it was obviously a derby game and it was an absolutely scorching hot day, it couldn't have gone more to plan.

My move to St Helens was for a record fee at the time for a forward. Warrington were great with me, and I'll never, ever have a bad word to say about the club. They gave me my opportunity and they really looked after me. It was never about financial gain, why I wanted to move. Warrington were struggling financially in regard to recruiting and strengthening the team to compete with the likes of Wigan and Saints. I had already broken into the Great Britain set-up, I was already playing with your top players in Super League, players who were playing in Challenge Cup Finals and winning championships and that's what I wanted. I just thought I would never do that at Warrington, certainly at that time. We had just sold Iestyn [Harris] to Leeds, which for me was a sign of a lack of ambition, because you don't sell your best young players. I asked for a meeting with the chairman and explained all that, he fully understood and he respected the way I had gone about it and granted my transfer request if someone paid the right fee for me.

I actually wasn't that far off signing for London Broncos; they came in for me when Richard Branson had just bought the club. They approached me first when it first went public; they flew me down to London in Richard's helicopter and we went to his house for dinner. I actually agreed personal terms there and then with the Broncos, but what was still to be done was the transfer request – but then Saints came in for me. I had always said that my only reason for leaving Warrington was to win things and Saints had just come off winning the Challenge Cup in 1996 and 1997 and I knew it was a place that I would get the opportunity to play in big games and win things.

I couldn't turn it down. I loved my time at St Helens. It was ten years of my life and I'm still involved with the club in an ambassadorial role. When I finished playing, I went into the commercial side, so the club has been a massive part of my life and Eamon McManus has always been great with me. I have a lot of good memories from my time with Saints. It's very difficult to pinpoint some of them because I have played so many games and a lot of good things happened to me at that club.

They were special times. It's hard to single out certain memories because we were always in contention to win things and playing in big games. Obviously the two World Club Challenge wins against Brisbane Broncos stand out because we came up against two top Brisbane sides littered with some of the best players in the world. To win those two games was pretty special. The one in 2007, I was coming back after six months out from injury. It was my first game back and I probably only had five days of training with the team, so that was a special moment to come back in a game like that and win the man of the match award and win the game against the Aussies.

I never questioned my ability and also my work ethic to come back. That Brisbane game in 2007, I was probably in the best shape I had ever been in during my career. Alright, yeah, I had not played in a while and you could be ring-rusty, but I think coming on as a substitute helped. Longy then asked me to do the goal-kicking when I came on, and I banged that one over from the touchline when Ade Gardner scored, and I just thought it was going to be one of those good days. Everything just went to plan.

The incident with Andy Farrell at Knowsley Road is something that always gets mentioned. Me and Faz are really good mates, obviously we played together many times. Not a lot of people know that we have been family friends from being kids. Andy's dad Peter actually coached me as a nine-year-old, so we grew up together and all the families are close. It was nothing boiling that led to it at all, all that was a case of Saints v Wigan and something goes off and you deal with it, and that's what we did. Our good friend Terry Newton started it, God bless his soul, as he usually did. He had a set-to with Wilko [Jon Wilkin] and we were just backing our team-mates up, as you do. Everyone knew we were good team-mates for Great Britain, and I was vice-captain to Andy, but that's the great thing about our game – what happens on the field stays on the field.

It's about those 80 minutes and getting on top of your opposition and doing everything you can to win the game. That was just a pure case of that. People said 'Did it go any further?' and it never went any further past that penalty being given. We had full respect for each other and probably walked off the field with our arms around each other.

My ambassadorial role is pretty much doing appearances for the club or whatever is required, like attending a few games or speaking at the matches. Sometimes it just helps to open doors; I have a great network of people and contacts, so it just opens a few doors for the club as well. I am not tied to any desk or any hours or anything like that, I am just representing the club when I can.

TOMMY MARTYN

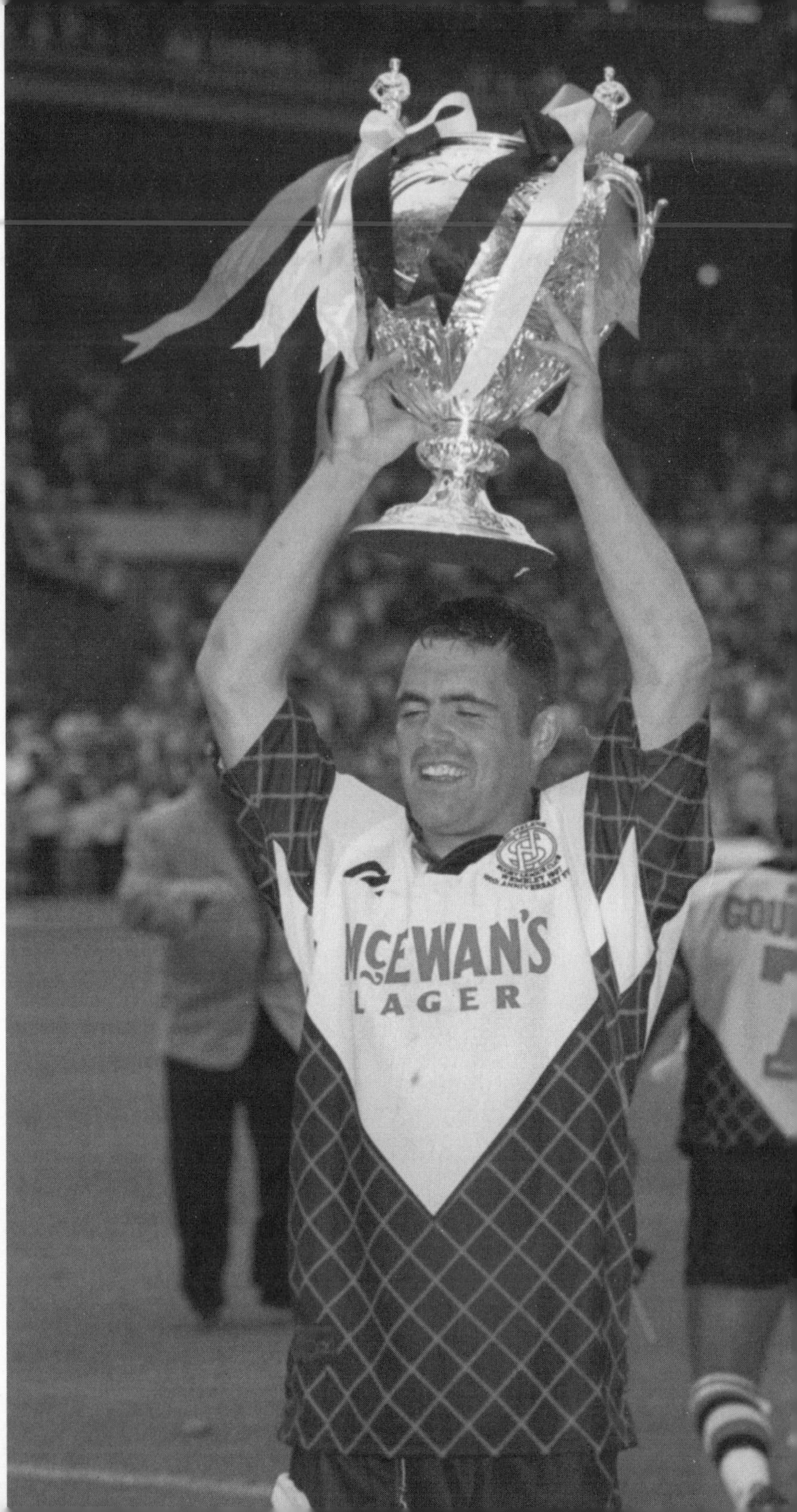

Tommy Martyn

STAND-OFF 1993–2003
HERITAGE NUMBER 1042

BORN: 4 June 1971, Leigh

SIGNED: 2 August 1993 from Oldham

DEBUT: 5 September 1993 vs Salford Red Devils

LAST GAME: 2 May 2003 vs Halifax

ST HELENS CAREER: 211 appearances (including 23 as a substitute), 127 tries, 105 goals, 24 drop goals

HONOURS: Super League 1996, 1999, 2000; Challenge Cup 1996, 1997, 2001; World Club Challenge 2001; League Leaders' Shield 2002

LEFT: 2003 to join Leigh Centurions

PLAYING CAREER: Oldham (1989–92), St Helens (1993–2003), Leigh Centurions (2003–04)

Tommy Martyn, or 'Tommy God' as he was affectionately known by the Knowsley Road faithful, joined the Saints from Oldham in 1994. He made his debut in the Red Vee against Salford at home and kicked four goals in a 22-14 victory.

Injuries are part and parcel of playing rugby league, but Martyn seemed to suffer more than others as he had to undergo two knee reconstructions, suffered three broken arms and four hernias. But when he was fully fit and out on the park, he was nearly unstoppable.

Martyn always seemed to turn on the style when the Saints played Wigan, not surprising seeing as he was from Leigh. He scored a hat-trick in a 30-28 win over the Warriors and he will go down in history as the last player to ever score a try at Central Park – something a lot of Wigan fans still cannot deal with.

Martyn's vision was first class; he could see a passage of play three tackles ahead of normal players and this was evident when he took full control of the Challenge Cup Final against Bradford Bulls in 1997.

That is the game that Martyn has chosen to remember and his partnership with Bobbie Goulding at Wembley was a joy to watch. Martyn also reveals how his move to St Helens came about and the devastation he felt when he was told he was no longer wanted at the club.

St Helens 32-22 Bradford Bulls
Challenge Cup Final
Saturday, 3 May 1997
Wembley Stadium, London
Attendance 78,022

Teams

St Helens	*Bradford Bulls*
Steve Prescott	Stuart Spruce
Danny Arnold	Abi Ekoku
Andy Haigh	Danny Peacock
Paul Newlove	Paul Loughlin
Anthony Sullivan	Paul Cook
Tommy Martyn	Graeme Bradley
Bobbie Goulding	Robbie Paul
Apollo Perelini	Brian McDermott
Keiron Cunningham	James Lowes
Julian O'Neill	Tahi Reihana
Chris Joynt	Sonny Nickle
Derek McVey	Bernard Dwyer
Karle Hammond	Steve McNamara

Subs

Chris Morley	Glen Tomlinson
Ian Pickavance	Paul Medley
Vila Matautia	Simon Knox
Andy Northey	Matt Calland

Coaches

Shaun McRae	Matthew Elliott

Tries

Martyn (2)	Loughlin
Hammond	Lowes
Joynt	Peacock
Sullivan	Tomlinson

Goals

Goulding (6)	McNamara (3)

Referee: Stuart Cummings

St Helens and Bradford Bulls had played out one of the best Challenge Cup Finals ever in 1996 when Bobbie Goulding and Robbie Paul both took centre stage for their respective teams.

One player who doesn't have the fondest memories from that game was Tommy Martyn. He had just come back from a knee reconstruction and was named on the bench, but early in the second half he picked up another knee injury and had to leave the field. Despite winning the game, Martyn vowed if he ever got to play at Wembley again, he would make it count.

He did that 12 months later as he scored two tries – off perfect Goulding kicks – while he also set up Chris Joynt for a crucial score as the Saints made it back-to-back Challenge Cup Final victories. It wasn't just in attack that Martyn shone at Wembley, he also put in a big shift in defence as he was named Lance Todd Trophy winner for the best player on the park.

Martyn was on top of the world, but in this chapter, he admits his world came crashing down just days later as he once again picked up a serious injury. Martyn insists he never once thought about quitting over injuries and he knew he had the will and determination to keep getting up off the floor to do his best for St Helens.

Back in the early nineties, Gary Connolly did the unthinkable and left Saints to join hated rivals Wigan. Still to this day, Connolly is booed and called Judas, but Martyn reveals here that if Connolly had stayed at St Helens, then they would never have seen him in a red V.

Having thought about my career at St Helens, I would have to say the 1997 Challenge Cup Final against Bradford Bulls [is my most memorable match]. I was substitute the year before, in 1996, it was touch and go whether or not I was going to play in that game at all because I had just come back from a knee reconstruction. I only played about four games under Shaun McRae heading into that 1996 final.

I managed to get on the bench for the 1996 Cup Final, but ten minutes into the second half I had to come off with another knee injury and I always vowed that if I ever got the chance to go back to Wembley, although I knew there were far better players than me who never got to play a single minute there, I would grab it with both hands. And fortunately for me and the team, we went back the following year. We were in a rich vein of form, I was playing well, and the team was going well, so we were very confident going into that Challenge Cup Final.

Bradford had signed Stuart Spruce to deal with our bombs, because if you remember Bobbie Goulding had bombed Nathan Graham a few times the year before. They thought they had it all covered, but in 1997 we decided to kick it along the floor. I remember just trying to take the whole occasion in, because everyone says to try and take it all in as it goes by in a flash, but it is very hard to do that. Nerves get in the way and things like that. I just remember early in the game, we went down the blind side, Bobbie came down the blind and dinked a little one through. I think it was the third or fourth tackle and there was a bit of a foot race between myself and Abi Ekoku, and I managed to get there before him and that helped us go 4-0 up.

Bradford hit back more or less straight away and they led 10-4 after Danny Peacock and Paul Loughlin both scored. Not long after, Bobbie came flashing from one side of the field, behind the ruck, took it to the line and I've always had a bit of an understanding with my half-back that if I'm far enough away I know they are not going to hit me, so I hoped he had the knowledge to just think, I can't hit him with a pass because he's seen something so I'll just slide it through and this is what Bobbie did to perfection yet again.

It was then a fiery ten-metre sprint between myself and Danny Peacock to get there. I just remember scoring two tries in a Challenge Cup Final, which went a long way to helping me win the Lance Todd Trophy for man of the match. It is certainly one of the proudest moments of my career. I'm not really sure that it kick-started my career, because four or five days after that I went playing for Ireland and snapped my other cruciate on my other leg. So, it didn't really kick-start it, it put me up there but then I came crashing down with an almighty bump.

Injuries are part and parcel of the game and I certainly had a fair few of them. You need a good support network, good friends and family around you. I was fortunate the first time it happened, I had Allan Hunte to do my rehab with because he had exactly the same injury. He was about three or four weeks in front of me. The second time, I knew what to do. Obviously, I was devastated. I was due to go in to have new contract talks with the board after winning the Lance Todd Trophy in that game at Wembley. Then to have my world come crashing down, it was a bitter pill to swallow, but at no point did I ever think about jacking it in. I knew I'd done it once so I knew I could do it again. It spurs you on; if you can come back from one knee reconstruction and win the Lance Todd Trophy at Wembley, then I'm sure you can do it a second time.

I loved playing rugby league, I always tried to play with a smile on my face because I had been there and worked in the dark days where you had to get up at 4am and drive a wagon all over the country and then get back for 6pm training and do it all again the next day. So, to be told that you were going to become a full-time professional athlete and do it for a living, that is what little kids dream of doing. There were certainly no full-time professional athletes [in rugby league] when I was growing up. You always had a second job on top of playing rugby. I have nothing but fond memories from my time at St Helens. We had gone from the nearly-men to being one of the teams to beat in Super League.

Everyone knows about the rivalry between St Helens and Wigan and we always had great games, but remember I am not from St Helens, I am from Leigh. There is no love lost between the people from Leigh and the people from Wigan, especially on the sporting field. To come to St Helens, people from St Helens think they hate Wigan, well Leigh people hate them even more. Don't get me wrong, we are never going to go into battle against them, but when you come to the derby games a Leigh lad can get just as fired up as a St Helens lad playing against Wigan. Any player, whether it's a Wigan player or a Saints player, gets fired up for a local derby. The juices get flowing, as soon as the game before gets out of the way then all you are thinking about is the following weekend against your biggest rivals. It's just fortunate that we always seemed to have a decent game.

Every one of us was fired up, but you just try and do something that little bit extra special and put that little bit more effort into the tackle. Fortunately, a few times, it just happened to come off for me. I loved playing against Wigan, I didn't actually realise at the time, that I had scored the last ever try at Central Park. I went out for a few beers afterwards with my mates, I basically went back to Leigh and went out and it was one of the landlords that said, 'Now then, what does it feel like to be the last person to ever score at Central Park?' Actually, I could have been the last person to ever kick a goal as well, but it hit the corner flag. I was nowhere near with that one.

My exit from St Helens was not a pleasant experience. I think my contract was up at the end of that season, but I had broken my arm for the third time. Instead of going in straight away and getting it plated, I wanted it to try and heal naturally. Later we had decided to go in and get it plated. It was while I was coming back, the coach said that I was no longer wanted at the club, which I found hard to take. They said they didn't think I was going to make a full recovery. The hardest part to take for me was after I had gone, they signed a prop from Warrington whose arm snapped during a bench press. It was double standards. It was a coach who I had really admired, and I had a lot of time for and he just went downhill after that in my estimation. I don't think I have spoken two words to him since, but it's just one of those things. I haven't spoken to anyone about it, it was the coach who didn't want me to stay. The board didn't want me to go, but as soon as a coach doesn't want you then there is no point in sticking around playing for someone who doesn't want you. When I had come back from broken arms before, I had won man of the matches and things like that, so it wasn't a case of my fitness or it had slowed me down, it was just a freak injury that hadn't healed properly and I had to have an operation to make it strong, but it's just one of those things.

A player never wants to be told he is not wanted; a player always wants to finish on his terms; unfortunately at Saints it didn't happen like that. If someone said to me when I was 22 years of age, 'You are going to be at Saints for ten years and you are going to win numerous Challenge Cups and Super League titles and also be crowned champions of the world,' I would have told them to shove it because I would never have believed them. To have the career I have had – don't get me wrong, it's not been easy, you have to put in the hard work and there's blood, sweat and tears along the way – but I would not swap one single minute of it.

How did my move to St Helens come about? I had played about four years at Oldham, Peter Tunks was the coach at the time and it was just getting ridiculous. In one season at Oldham, we ended up using 52 players. No one ever knew who was going to be your half-back partner or your centre or your winger, it was like the *Multi-Coloured Swap Shop*. I just got fed up after being there for four years doing quite a bit of travelling, and I put a transfer request in. Tunksy said, 'If I can get you away I will,' and fortunately out of the blue one night, I got a phone call from a director at St Helens saying they were going to put a bid in for me. But the only way they could do it was when Gary Connolly had gone to Wigan. So, I was probably the only person in rugby league who wanted Gary to go to Wigan so I could get my move to St Helens. I had heard a rumour the year before that Saints were sniffing around with me, Sonny Nickle and Chris Joynt, but there was more demand for Joynty and Sonny, so they went for them first.

APOLLO PERELINI

Apollo Perelini

PROP FORWARD 1994–2000
HERITAGE NUMBER 1054

BORN: 16 July 1969, Auckland, New Zealand

SIGNED: 3 June 1994 from North Harbour RU

DEBUT: 11 September 1994 vs Workington Town

LAST GAME: 14 October 2000 vs Wigan Warriors

ST HELENS CAREER: 193 appearances (including 30 as a substitute), 44 tries

HONOURS: Challenge Cup 1996, 1997; Super League 1996, 1999, 2000

LEFT: 2000 to join Sale Sharks

PLAYING CAREER: Auckland RU (1990–92), North Harbour RU (1992–94), St Helens (1994–2000), Sale Sharks (2000–04)

Apollo Perelini arrived in St Helens as a relative unknown, but by the time he left the club in 2000, he was a household name and a legend of the club.

Perelini made the switch from rugby union in the summer of 1994 and during his time at the club it is not an exaggeration to say he was one of the greatest front-rowers to ever wear the Red Vee. His first two seasons saw them fail to win any silverware, but the Regal Trophy Final defeat against Wigan in

1995 lit a fire under everyone at St Helens and the switch to summer rugby saw Perelini and his team-mates step up to the plate as they won the double.

St Helens were unable to successfully defend their Super League title in 1997, but they did make it back-to-back Challenge Cup victories over Bradford Bulls at Wembley. Perelini added two more Super League titles to his honours list with his final official game for the club coming in their 29-16 win over Wigan in the 2000 Grand Final at Old Trafford.

Perelini has opted for the 1996 Challenge Cup Final success as his greatest game at St Helens. He reveals how they refused to panic and self-destruct when it looked like Bradford were going to take a stranglehold on the final.

The prop forward scored the crucial try that kept the Saints clear of the Bulls as they lifted the Challenge Cup for the first time since they beat Wigan back in 1966.

Perelini left the club to return to rugby union with Sale Sharks at the end of the 2000 campaign, but he did return to the club in 2004 when he took on the role of their fitness conditioner. During his time on the coaching staff, Perelini helped the Saints to one Grand Final win, four Challenge Cup victories and one World Club Championship title.

St Helens 40-32 Bradford Bulls
Challenge Cup Final
Saturday, 27 April 1996
Wembley Stadium, London
Attendance 78,550

Teams

St Helens	*Bradford Bulls*
Steve Prescott	Nathan Graham
Danny Arnold	Paul Cook
Scott Gibbs	Matt Calland
Paul Newlove	Paul Loughlin
Anthony Sullivan	Jon Scales
Karle Hammond	Graeme Bradley
Bobbie Goulding	Robbie Paul
Apollo Perelini	Brian McDermott
Keiron Cunningham	Bernard Dwyer
Andy Leathem	Jon Hamer
Chris Joynt	Jeremy Donougher
Simon Booth	Sonny Nickle
Andy Northey	Simon Knox

Subs

Tommy Martyn	Karl Fairbank
Ian Pickavance	Paul Medley
Vila Matautia	Jason Donohue
Alan Hunte	Carlos Hassan

Coaches

Shaun McRae	Brian Smith

Tries

Arnold (2)	Paul (3)
Prescott (2)	Dwyer
Booth	Scales
Cunningham	
Perelini	
Pickavance	

Goals

Goulding (4)	Cook (6)

Referee: Stuart Cummings

The 1996 Challenge Cup Final was St Helens' first visit to Wembley since going down 13-8 to Wigan in 1991, while this was Bradford's first Cup Final appearance since losing 33-14 in 1973.

This final will go down as one of the greatest Challenge Cup Finals ever. In the second half, it looked like St Helens had run out of steam after they had dominated early on.

Bradford led 14-12 at the break, while Robbie Paul and Bernard Dwyer both scored to put the Yorkshire side 26-12 ahead. St Helens refused to panic and the game changed dramatically in the space of ten minutes when Bobbie Goulding kicked the Bulls to death with Keiron Cunningham, Simon Booth and Ian Pickavance all capitalising as Saints hit the front at 30-26.

Danny Arnold and Robbie Paul then traded tries, with the latter being the first player to ever score a hat-trick in a Challenge Cup Final. Saints led 34-32 heading into the last five minutes until Perelini took a switch pass from Goulding to storm over under the posts to see St Helens lift the Challenge Cup for the first time in 20 years.

Perelini highlights the fact that his team-mates refused to panic when the pressure was on and that was the catalyst for them securing the double in the first ever Super League season. He also reveals that he was reluctant to ever face off against St Helens, which is one of the reasons he went back to rugby union once his time with the Saints was up.

The game that stands out more than most during my time at St Helens has to be the 1996 Challenge Cup Final at Wembley Stadium against Bradford Bulls. It was such an honour to be a part of such a prestige game; we were all up for this one.

It was an exciting build-up to the Challenge Cup Final as we travelled down to London on the Thursday morning with a great send-off from at least a few hundred supporters who came down to the club to see us off.

We had not been in the final for a few years and it had been 20 years since St Helens had last lifted the Challenge Cup trophy. So, there was an air of excitement and a sheer buzz of confidence travelling down to London.

The occasion was amazing, to be able to play in a game like the Challenge Cup Final is something I will never forget. The game itself, well it was very fast and we got out of the blocks really fast with two quick tries from Steve Prescott in the opening 15 minutes.

We looked in control, but Bradford Bulls were a great team themselves and they struck back and before we knew it, we were 14-12 down at half-time. When former St Helens hooker and fans' favourite Bernard Dwyer scored after half-time, we all got together behind the posts and made an agreement as a team that we were not to be concerned with the score or the outcome. But instead we were going to start focusing on the simple processes of keeping hold of the ball and getting down the field. Once we got down Bradford's end, Bobbie Goulding was going to start putting the ball up and our job was to put pressure on the receiver.

Basically, that is how we got back into the game, we regained our composure and clawed our way back. It's a game you will never really forget, because it is still credited with being one of the greatest comebacks in the history of the Challenge Cup.

The game was heading into the closing moments and we were only a try in front with four minutes left on the clock. We continued to put pressure on the Bradford defence and we entered their 22. I called out to Bobbie to hand me the ball, so he ran across field and gave me the ball on the switch and I made my way under the posts for the winning try and helped lift the famous trophy.

The best part of that Challenge Cup Final win at Wembley in 1996 was the celebrations that went on in the town of St Helens on our return from London. The streets were lined with thousands of supporters as we returned home with the Challenge Cup for the first time in 20 years.

That 1996 Challenge Cup Final was the best game of my career with regards to team passion and sheer grit to fight for each other irrespective of the score. We went on to win some very crucial matches that we looked like losing, but through the confidence of the players with each other, we were able to grind out wins that we shouldn't have. London Broncos away is another game that will live long in the memory. My try with the ball above my head that the video referee seemed to take forever in deciding and the tough win away at Castleford near the end of the season are two of the reasons why we were a very successful team.

We were only one point ahead of Wigan in the league table and the inaugural Super League championship was to be decided on the final game of the season against Warrington Wolves at Knowsley Road. The team was very confident going into this final home game. We were on fire that day, we blew Warrington away 66-14 with Alan Hunte scoring a hat-trick of tries, while Paul Newlove, Anthony Sullivan and Tommy Martyn scored two tries each as we were crowned champions.

The great thing about my departure from the club was that St Helens remains the only rugby league club that I have ever played for in my whole career. When I left the club, I left to go to rugby union as it would have been difficult playing against St Helens with another rugby league club. I was in my early thirties and wanted to give my remaining rugby life back in the sport I had started from, which was rugby union, and signing for Sale Sharks in Manchester meant I didn't have to uproot my young family and I could still live in my adopted home town of St Helens.

PAUL LOUGHLIN

Paul Loughlin

FULL-BACK/CENTRE 1983–95
HERITAGE NUMBER 967

BORN: 28 July 1966, St Helens

SIGNED: 8 August 1983 from St Helens Colts

DEBUT: 1 April 1984 vs Oldham

LAST GAME: 26 November 1995 vs Hull

ST HELENS CAREER: 297 appearances (including 11 as a substitute), 80 tries, 842 goals

HONOURS: John Player Special Trophy 1988; Premiership Trophy 1993

LEFT: 1995 to join Bradford Bulls

PLAYING CAREER: St Helens (1983–95), Bradford Bulls (1995–97), Huddersfield Giants (1998–99), Swinton Lions (2000–01)

Paul Loughlin joined St Helens as a teenager after impressing in the Colts team; he soon became a household name and went on to play just under 300 games for the club, scoring 80 tries and kicking 842 goals.

During his time at Saints, Loughlin won the John Player Special Trophy and the Premiership Trophy in 1988 and 1993 respectively, before being offloaded to Bradford Bulls before the start of the inaugural Super League season, along with Sonny Nickle and Bernard Dwyer in a move that saw Paul Newlove move to Knowsley Road.

That victory over Leeds in the 1987–88 John Player Special Trophy Final is the game Loughlin has chosen as his best game in the Red Vee. He admits that picking one match out of nearly 300 was exceedingly difficult but having scored 14 points out of 15 in the win he says it was difficult to overlook that achievement.

When recalling the final, Loughlin has to chuckle at the fact that he got the man of the match award at Central Park and scored 14 points in the 15-14 success over Leeds, but all the headlines in the newspaper the following day just fixated on the man who scored one point.

St Helens 15-14 Leeds
John Player Trophy Final
Saturday, 9 January 1988
Central Park, Wigan
Attendance 16,669

Teams
St Helens   *Leeds*
Phil Veivers   Marty Gurr
Dave Tanner   Steve Morris
Paul Loughlin   Gary Schofield
Mark Elia   Peter Jackson
Les Quirk   John Basnett
Shane Cooper   David Creasser
Neil Holding   Ray Ashton
Tony Burke   Peter Tunks
Paul Groves   Colin Maskill
Peter Souto   Kevin Rayne
Paul Forber   Roy Powell
Roy Haggerty   Paul Medley
Andy Platt   David Heron

Subs
David Large   Carl Gibson
Stuart Evans   John Fairbank

Coaches
Alex Murphy   Maurice Bamford

Tries
Loughlin (2)   Creasser
                                   Jackson

Goals
Loughlin (3)   Creasser (3)
Drop goal
Holding

Referee: Fred Lindop

The 1987–88 John Player Special Trophy Final was the 17th of its kind and just under 17,000 people made their way to Wigan's Central Park ground to witness the Saints win their first piece of silverware since they won both the Premiership trophy and the Lancashire Cup in 1984–85.

The final was a closely contested one, with Neil Holding's drop goal just before the half-time break separating the two teams after 80 minutes. But it was the performance of Paul Loughlin that everyone really remembers – well maybe not the headline writers.

Loughlin walked away with a personal tally of 14 points thanks to two tries and three goals. Saints were trailing 14-9 before Loughlin went over for his second try. He converted his own effort to put them 15-14 in front and it was a lead they never let go of.

As well as playing for Saints, Loughlin will always be remembered for his performances in a Great Britain shirt. He made his Lions debut in 1988 and ended up on the Ashes tour to Australia. He was named as centre in the third and final Test and made an amazing break down the right to send Henderson Gill in for his now famous 'boogie' try. He also scored a fine interception try for Great Britain in the second Test of the 1990 series in Australia.

During this chapter, Loughlin reveals the moment his time at St Helens came to an end. He went in to see the chairman thinking he was going to be handed a new car after agreeing a new deal for the start of Super League, only to be told he was going to be used as a pawn in the move to get Paul Newlove to join St Helens.

Loughlin wanted to stay at Saints, but he was told he would just end up playing A team rugby for the rest of his contract. He agreed to move to Bradford and ended up playing in two Challenge Cup Final defeats against Saints, as well as winning the Super League in 1997.

I've had a few great games for Saints: the comeback win against Wigan will always be special, but the one that sticks in my mind for me, was when we played Leeds in the John Player Special Trophy Final in 1988 at Central Park.

Leeds had around four internationals in their team; they had Marty Gurr at full-back, Gary Schofield was in the side, David Creasser and Peter Jackson, who isn't with us anymore, Roy Powell, who is also not with us anymore … the list could go on. They had a really great team back then.

We had a few players missing for this final, but we ended up winning the game 15-14. It was a really good game. Imagine playing in January on that heavy pitch at Central Park, it was hard work. I remember Andy Platt doing about 50 tackles and I think I did about three, but what made it special was that I got two tries and three goals and got 14 of our points and I got man of the match as well. That performance probably got me on the Great Britain tour to be honest, but Neil Holding dropped a goal and we won the game. On the Sunday, I went to pick up the newspapers and all the headlines said was 'Holding Wins It for Saints'. So that was funny actually; I scored 14 out of 15 points and the other guy gets the plaudits.

Out of all the years I was at Saints and the amount of games I played in, I would have to say that was the one that really stands out in my mind. That game kind of got me recognised as a good player, especially in the selectors' eyes as I was selected to play for Great Britain. I made my debut not long after and then I was selected to go on the Great Britain tour of Australia in 1988. It was probably that game that made them come to the decision of thinking I was good enough to go on tour. Looking back on that tour, no one gave us a chance really. We all had a go, on another day some of the passes and the runs might have come off and we might have won the Ashes. But that third Test, everything seemed to click on that one day. It was the first time we had beaten Australia over there for a few years, I know the win didn't win us the Ashes and it was just a Test match but it was still a great feeling and they always show that try where I made the break and Henderson Gill went in at the corner and did a bit of a 'boogie'. That's what everyone remembers about that game.

How did I end up at Saints? I was about 16 and my dad had started an under-17 team because there were a few players that Saints were after like Shaun Allen and Dave Lee. Shaun was like the Shaun Edwards of the St Helens team; he was signed on his birthday and they kept it quiet and then he started playing first team. So, I was playing in my dad's team and then I started to play for the Colts team on a Saturday. Then it kicked on from there really, when I was 17 I signed on with Saints.

There were a few of us that signed at the same time as there were a few good lads coming through at that time. I was at Saints for about 12 and a half years, the game is miles different now to when I started. You had the first team, the A team and the Colts. Those A team games were some of the most ferocious ones I have ever been involved in, because all the players were looking to prove a point. You had players who had been left out of the first team looking to get their place back, and you had young lads trying to make a name for themselves, plus don't forget lads coming back from injury as well. You were also playing for a bit of money, in those days you got winning and losing money so as well as trying to earn a pay packet you also had a chance of being called up as a reserve for the first team if you played well. People were willing to rip players' heads off just to get a few extra quid. That wasn't just at Saints, that was every club.

How did my time at Saints come to an end? I had signed a contract for the first Super League season with Saints, and then I got a call off the chairman to see if I would come back to the club for a talk. I didn't think much about it; actually I had asked for a car, so I thought I was going to be given a car. But when I got there, I could see Bernard [Dwyer] and Sonny [Nickle]. Bernard was made up because Bradford had come in and they wanted me, Bernard and Sonny and they wanted Paul Newlove to come to Saints in exchange for us and money. He was made up, Bernard – basically Bradford had offered him what he was on at Saints with a three-year deal and a car and everything, so he was happy. Actually, it was probably a good move for all of us really financially. I was a bit gutted that my time at Saints had come to an end, but I spoke to the chairman and asked him if I didn't leave, what would actually happen. He told me they had signed Scott Gibbs and they were going to sign Paul Newlove anyway, so I would probably be playing A team rugby. It was one of them things, there was nothing I could do really. I wasn't the first and I certainly won't be the last player to be shown the door that way, but it was a good move for both clubs.

Obviously, Saints did well with Newlove and Bradford did well with all three lads that went there. They took me, Bernard and Sonny and we were seen as older players that other teams didn't want, but it worked with Bradford. I ended up getting to two more Challenge Cup Finals at Wembley and winning Super League during my time there. Apart from the two Wembley finals, losing against Saints twice hurt, but there are a lot better players than me that never got the chance to play at Wembley in a Challenge Cup Final, so I will always be grateful for that.

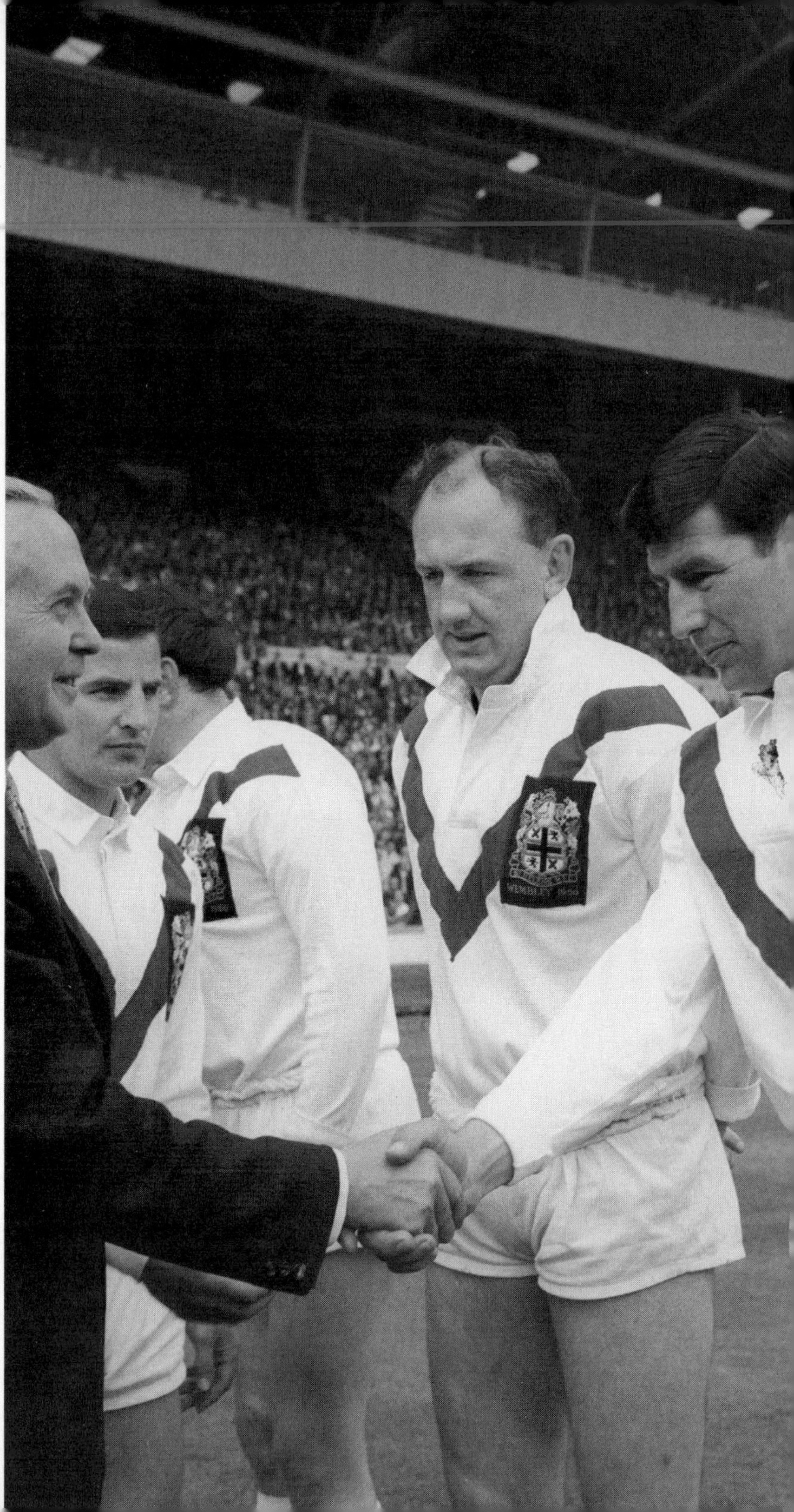
WEMBLEY 1966

Ray French

SECOND ROW 1961–67
HERITAGE NUMBER 786

BORN: 23 December 1939, St Helens

SIGNED: Date unknown from St Helens Rugby Union

DEBUT: 30 August 1961 vs Wakefield Trinity

LAST GAME: 28 August 1967 vs Wakefield Trinity

ST HELENS CAREER: 204 appearances (including 3 as a substitute), 10 tries

HONOURS: Lancashire Cup 1961, 1963; 1964, Challenge Cup 1966; League Championship 1966; Western Division Championship 1964; Lancashire League 1965, 1966, 1967

LEFT: 1967 to join Widnes

PLAYING CAREER: St Helens (1961–67), Widnes (1967–71)

Ray French is like royalty in St Helens. Whenever he speaks, people listen. That was how he rolled as a player and it continued into his later career as a rugby league commentator.

French joined his local side in 1961 from the town's rugby union side and went on to make over 200 appearances for the Saints in his six-season spell. He was a no-nonsense second-row forward, who never took a backward step, and earned the respect of not only his team-mates, but his opponents as well.

He may have only scored ten tries during his Saints career, but that doesn't reflect his whole career. He was an invaluable member of the St Helens team and is still loved by many today.

A lot of fans reading this may only remember French as a commentator, and it's fair to say he was a joy to listen to. He might be remembered for little quips like 'Kett Kenny' and 'he can run this f...hooker', but his voice always makes me remember the Challenge Cup Finals of yesteryear and the international matches between Great Britain and Australia.

French was part of my childhood growing up, in terms of rugby league, and not only will he always be known as a legend in St Helens, he is also a rugby league legend throughout the whole world.

St Helens 21-2 Wigan
Challenge Cup Final
Saturday, 21 May 1966
Wembley Stadium, London
Attendance 98,536

Teams
St Helens

Frank Barrow
Tom van Vollenhoven
Alex Murphy
Billy Benyon
Len Killeen
Peter Harvey
Tommy Bishop
Albert Halsall
Bill Sayer
Cliff Watson
Ray French
John Warlow
John Mantle

Subs
Tony Barrow
Jeff Hitchen

Coaches
Joe Coan

Wigan

Ray Ashby
Billy Boston
David Stephens
Eric Ashton
Trevor Lake
Cliff Hill
Frank Parr
Danny Gardiner
Tom Woosey
Brian McTigue
Tony Stephens
Laurie Gilfedder
Harry Major

None used

Eric Ashton

Tries
Bishop
Killeen
Mantle

Goals
Killeen (5)   Gilfedder

Drop Goal
Murphy

Referee: H.G Hunt

When St Helens and Wigan play each other in a major final, it is always a huge deal, and the Challenge Cup Final in 1966 was no different. Saints outsmarted Wigan that day and lifted the trophy thanks to a 21-2 win.

My own dad was at this game as a Wigan fan with his aunty and uncle and whenever this game gets mentioned, he just says 'Yeah, the final Murphy cheated.'

Cheat might be a strong word, but it's true that Murphy used the rules to his benefit. Back in those days, if you got a penalty and kicked to touch, the game was restarted with a scrum rather than a tap as we see today.

St Helens had signed hooker Bill Sayer from Wigan after he lost his place to Colin Clarke. Clarke then found himself suspended for the Challenge Cup Final with Tom Woosey wearing the number nine jersey. Murphy proceeded to stand offside and then allow Sayer to hook the ball against the head every time Wigan kicked to touch.

It was clever thinking on the part of Murphy and that was instrumental in Saints beating Wigan for the second time in five years at Wembley Stadium. Heading into the final minutes of the game, Saints were leading 19-2 and the game was over as a contest. But Murphy was not satisfied with that as he added a drop goal to rub salt in Wigan's wounds.

Also, in this chapter, French goes into detail about the Saints v Wigan rivalry. According to French, the rivalry back in the sixties was more intense than it is today. He admits beating Wigan was all they wanted to do, and vice versa. Although the rivalry was fierce, French insists there was a healthy respect between the two as well.

The game I would have to choose as the standout of my St Helens career has to be the 1966 Challenge Cup Final against Wigan at Wembley Stadium. That has to be the game for me. We had played each other a couple of times during the season and we were very evenly matched.

Wigan had a fine side in 1966, they had the likes of Billy Boston, Eric Ashton, Brian McTigue and Laurie Gilfedder. Wigan had a class side but remember so did we. We had the likes of Frank Barrow, Tom van Vollenhoven, Alex Murphy, Len Killeen, Bill Sayer and Cliff Watson. So, these were two very good teams battling it out for the Challenge Cup.

To me, we had the better pack. Our pack was bigger and stronger, Watson, John Warlow and John Mantle were brilliant players to have in your team. One thing you need to remember about that 1996 Challenge Cup Final, Wigan had no hooker. Colin Clarke was their hooker and he was suspended, and they had to use Tom Woosey. In those days, we had proper scrums and we commanded the ball. Our hooker was Bill Sayer, who we signed from Wigan, and he won every scrum.

I wasn't the captain that day, it was Alex, but I was doing enough shouting. We were given a penalty in the early minutes of the game; it was way out. I actually think it was even in our own half. I said to Lenny Killeen, because he was a brilliant kicker, 'Lenny, can you kick this?' 'Yes,' he said, and Murph is going mad saying, 'No, no, put it to touch, put it to touch.' I said, 'Lenny, can you definitely kick this?' If he didn't kick the goal and he got the ball dead, we would get the ball back anyway. He took the ball and kicked it from over 50 yards, what a kick it was. It was probably the best goal kick ever to be seen at Wembley.

That put us in control, we got on top of them and then we kicked another goal. That really set us off, just to get that little lead of four points really made the difference. Although Wigan did come on strong at one time during that first half, we never really looked back. We had the pack to dominate the game, they lacked possession. We kept them try-less, which as a forward is always pleasing, as Tommy Bishop, Killeen and Mantle all crossed over as we blew Wigan away in the end.

The rivalry back then was massive, probably more so than it is today. Either side would rather lose any game than the one between Wigan and Saints. It sounds like a cliché, but it was true. It was quite funny to be honest, when you went from Saints' ground, which was Knowsley Road in those days, and you got on the coach. By the time you got halfway through Billinge, everybody was waving at you. By the time you got through Billinge, everybody was giving you the V signs. That was the atmosphere.

You would regularly be playing in front of at least 30,000 fans when Saints and Wigan played each other. No question about that. Whether it be Good Friday or Boxing Day, the fans would come out in force and the atmosphere was electric. Those were the games you really wanted to play in. I remember one Saints fan was being interviewed, he said to the press lad: 'You need to interview my dad, he'll tell you a story that is true.' So, this journalist found out who his dad was and where he lived and said, 'Your lad tells me you have a story to tell me.' This dad then said, 'When I go to Wigan to watch Saints and Wigan at Central Park, when I get home, I burn my shoes.' He must have had plenty of shoes, that's all I can say. But that was the kind of rivalry it was.

I do have to say, although it was the greatest of rivalries, it was also a great friendship as well between the two teams. Eric Ashton was a great friend of mine, and I got on so well with Billy Boston. Even though, to tackle Billy was like running into a truck. He was so powerful, and you really had to grab him to stop him. David Bolton was another fine player and Brian McTigue was superb. You would play 80 minutes, then you would be sat next to Brian in the bar afterwards, you'd been knocking hell out of each other all game, but you would be as happy as Larry together. It was a very good relationship between Saints and Wigan back then. The rivalry was fierce, but the respect was always there.

I loved my time at Saints. I had six really enjoyable years at the club. We won every trophy you could possibly win throughout those years. In fact, in 1966 we won the lot. I had the opportunity to play with some of the finest players to ever play the game of rugby league. In the pack alongside me, were the likes of Vince Karalius, Dick Huddart, Cliff Watson, and we played behind the likes of Alex Murphy, the great Tom van Vollenhoven the South African winger, Lenny Killeen, you name it, Austin Rhodes. You couldn't speak too highly of those kinds of players. The whole squad was class and I will always have fond memories of that time.

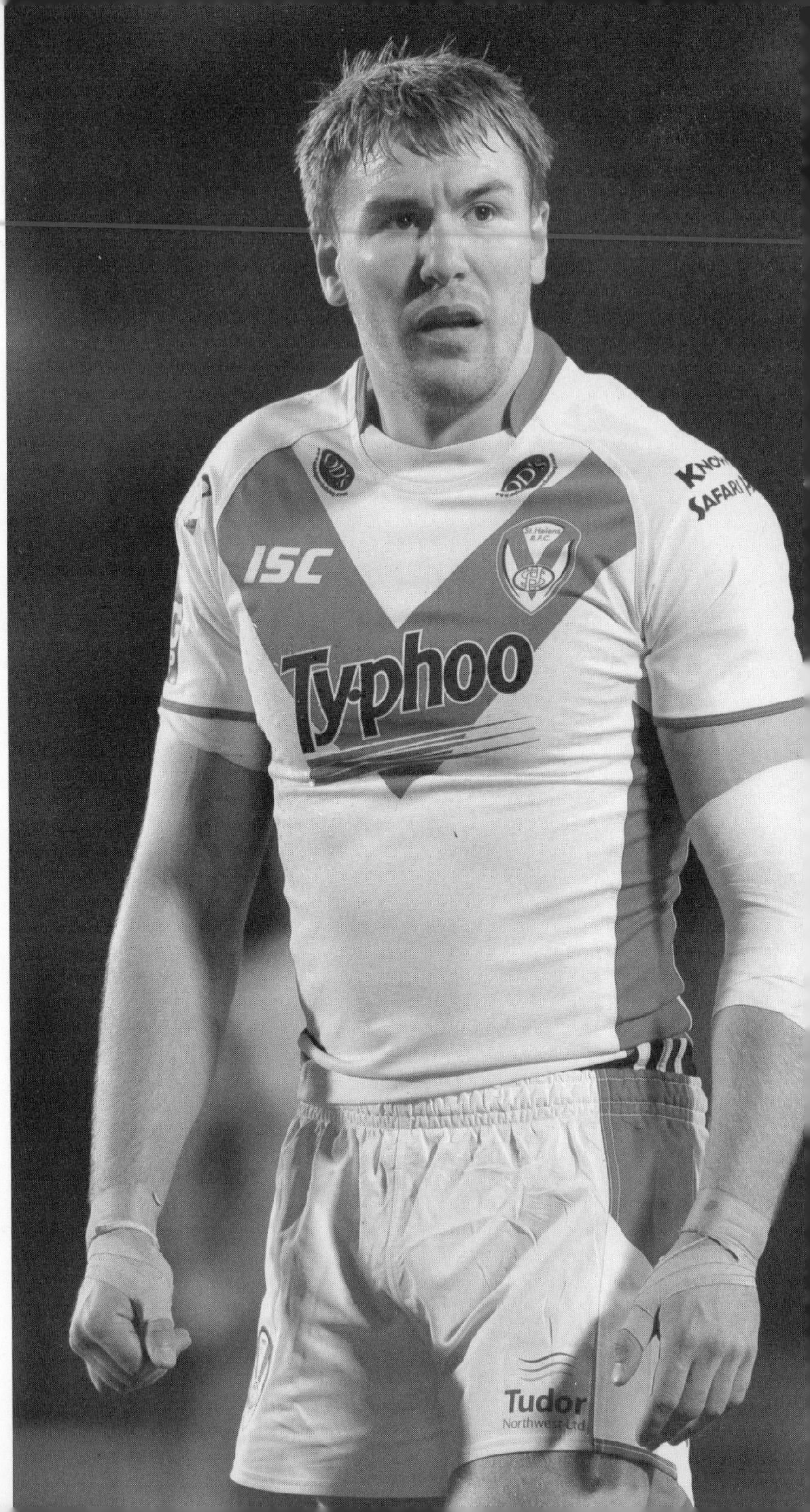

MICHAEL SHENTON

Michael Shenton

CENTRE 2011–12
HERITAGE NUMBER 1185

BORN: 22 July 1986, Pontefract

SIGNED: Date unknown from Castleford Tigers

DEBUT: 12 February 2011 vs Wigan Warriors

LAST GAME: 7 September 2012 vs Wigan Warriors

ST HELENS CAREER: 56 appearances, 20 tries

HONOURS: None

LEFT: 2012 to join Castleford Tigers

PLAYING CAREER: Castleford Tigers (2004–10), St Helens (2011–12), Castleford Tigers (2013–present)

Michael Shenton was already an England international when he moved to St Helens after seven years with Castleford Tigers.

Following the conclusion of his contract with the Tigers, Shenton moved across the Pennines and joined St Helens on a three-year contract.

Shenton only managed to play for two years at Saints before securing a move back to Castleford Tigers – where he is still plying his trade today.

Shenton played 56 times for the Saints during his brief spell and crossed over for 20 tries. He may not have won any silverware during his time with St Helens, but he still has fond memories of his time and fully appreciates how he was treated by everyone at the club – including the fans.

Despite not winning the Grand Final or Challenge Cup, Shenton played in some big games and the one he has chosen for this book is when Saints beat fierce rivals Wigan to reach the 2011 Grand Final.

St Helens 26-18 Wigan Warriors
Super League Play-Off Semi-Final
Saturday, 1 October 2011
Stobart Stadium, Widnes
Attendance 9,421

Teams

St Helens	*Wigan Warriors*
Paul Wellens	Sam Tomkins
Tommy Makinson	Josh Charnley
Michael Shenton	Joel Tomkins
Francis Meli	George Carmont
Jamie Foster	Pat Richards
Lee Gaskell	Brett Finch
Jonny Lomax	Tommy Leuluai
James Graham	Jeff Lima
James Roby	Michael McIlorum
Tony Puletua	Andy Coley
Sia Soliola	Harrison Hansen
Jon Wilkin	Ryan Hoffman
Paul Clough	Sean O'Loughlin

Subs

Scott Moore	Paul Prescott
Louie McCarthy-Scarsbrook	Eamon O'Carroll
Gary Wheeler	Liam Farrell
Andrew Dixon	Chris Tuson

Coaches

Royce Simmons	Michael Maguire

Tries

Gaskell	Charnley
Wellens	O'Carroll
Foster	S Tomkins
Roby	

Goals

Foster (5)	Richards (3)

Referee: Phil Bentham

St Helens ended the 2011 regular Super League season in third place with a points total of 37 having won 17 of their 27 matches. They finished behind second-anked Wigan Warriors and League Leaders' Shield winners Warrington Wolves.

That third-place finish saw the Saints have to travel to the DW Stadium to take on Wigan in the qualifying final that would see the winner advance to the semi-finals and the loser having a second chance in the preliminary semi-finals.

The Saints won 26-18 away from home with Paul Wellens grabbing a brace of tries. They were now just 80 minutes away from their sixth consecutive Grand Final appearance. Wigan won their preliminary final against Catalans Dragons and had to travel to Widnes' Stobart Stadium – Saints' home ground for that season – to battle it out for the right to face Leeds Rhinos at Old Trafford.

The Saints ran out 26-18 winners over the Warriors for the second game running, thanks to tries from Wellens, Jamie Foster, Lee Gaskell and James Roby.

Shenton admits that win was the biggest of his career at that time, and he will never forget the feeling of elation and relief once the final hooter sounded.

I think I ended up playing 56 games for St Helens, during the two years I spent at the club. Looking back on those games, the Grand Final was pretty special because that was my first major game in 2011, but the semi-final beforehand, beating Wigan to get there, was a pretty special game and one I will never forget.

We were on a real roll at that moment, we had been quite consistent throughout the season but it was the back end of that season where we really came into our own. Winning that semi-final was really special to me; we just had the determination and it came off for us and we deserved our place in the Grand Final a week later.

The game was actually played at Widnes. Langtree Park was still getting built at the time, so all our home matches were played at Widnes. I remember during the game Joel Tomkins ran the ball at me and I tackled him and I damaged my shoulder. It was killing, I was in a lot of trouble but refused to show any weakness. That was how tough we had to be to do it. I was in a lot of pain, but I kept on going because we knew there was a Grand Final at stake.

We kind of dominated the game to be honest, it seems a very long time ago now when you are looking back on it. When the final whistle went it was pure elation. It was elation and relief and a kind of surreal feeling that we had reached the Grand Final. Those were the initial feelings, but once we had got in the changing rooms, we knew we had to get ready mentally. We only had a week to prepare for the final, so you couldn't really celebrate as the main prize was just around the corner.

We had to get ready for a week of build-up and be involved in everything that goes on leading up to the

Grand Final at Old Trafford, all the preparation and the media side of it, sorting tickets out as well. All those things you have never really thought about. There is a lot going on, but we had a group of players there that reaching finals was second nature to because they had played in that many Grand Finals. That helped us really, because it helped us remain calm and focused. They were so calm because they had done it before and they had a lot of motivation going into it because they were so desperate to win one after the previous years where Saints had been beaten. But unfortunately, it was a game too far and we didn't come away with the win.

In my career at that time, I had represented my country as well which was massively important to me, but on the club side of my career that semi-final and Grand Final were the biggest games of my career. I'm not really sure how the move to St Helens came about really, I don't know if they had been tracking me for a while or not. I just know that my contract was coming to an end at Castleford and Saints were interested, and obviously they are an amazing club. The brand of rugby they play is exciting and the kind of players they already had at the club, I knew a couple like James Graham, Jon Wilkin and James Roby through playing for England, so I knew I had a few friends there which helped make the move a lot easier.

I had obviously never played in a Saints v Wigan derby before joining Saints, but I used to watch the

Good Friday games and you could see the intensity and the rivalry involved and I was looking forward to playing in those kinds of matches. You always feel under pressure to play well against Wigan, because everyone at the club wants you to beat them. It was an amazing game to be involved in though, my first St Helens v Wigan derby was absolutely incredible. The DW Stadium was packed out with both sets of fans, it was an amazing experience. All the Saints fans had turned up in their numbers and filled the away end, then the Wigan fans had really bought into it as well. You could see what it meant to everyone; there is just a different feel to those kinds of matches.

The fans at St Helens are great, they have always been good to me. I go back now as a Castleford player and they still give me a great reception. It's an incredible club with a fantastic history and you can tell they are in the rugby league heartland. They have plenty of young kids coming through now and they are just a very supportive club and a great place to play for.

TOMMY MAKINSON

Tommy Makinson

WING/FULL-BACK 2011–present
HERITAGE NUMBER 1187

BORN: 10 October 1991, Ince, Wigan

SIGNED: Date unknown from Wigan St Judes

DEBUT: 18 February 2011 vs Salford Red Devils

ST HELENS CAREER: 235 appearances (including 6 as a substitute), 133 tries, 124 goals, 1 drop goal

HONOURS: Super League 2014, 2019; League Leaders' Shield 2014, 2018, 2019

LEFT: Still at the club

PLAYING CAREER: St Helens (2011–present)

Tommy Makinson might have been born in Wigan and played his amateur rugby in the town, but the supporters of St Helens have well and truly claimed him as one of their own.

Makinson, who made his Saints debut in 2011 against Salford Red Devils, has become one of the best finishers in the game. His all-round game has come on over the years, and despite having some serious concerns, he has overcome every injury he has picked up and come back a better player.

St Helens won the League Leaders' Shield in 2014, but the icing on the cake came at Old Trafford when Makinson scored the winning try as the Saints defeated the old enemy – Wigan – in the Grand Final that will always be remembered for a moment of madness from Warriors prop forward Ben Flower.

Makinson has always insisted that he is in rugby league to win trophies as a team; individual honours are nice but he insists they will always come second to lifting the Super League trophy or Challenge Cup with his team-mates.

Despite saying that, he won the Golden Boot award in 2018 as the best international player in the world. The winger beat off competition from Elliott Whitehead, Dallin Watene-Zelezniak and James Tedesco to become the fifth Englishman to ever win the award after Ellery Hanley, Garry Schofield, Andy Farrell and Kevin Sinfield.

Makinson's career is far from over and since I have been writing this book, he has already added another Super League title to his list of achievements. Whenever fans name a team of St Helens greats in the future, then Makinson's name will most definitely be amongst them.

St Helens 14-6 Wigan Warriors

Super League Grand Final
Saturday, 11 October 2014
Old Trafford, Manchester
Attendance 70,102

Teams

St Helens	*Wigan Warriors*
Paul Wellens	Matty Bowen
Tommy Makinson	Josh Charnley
Mark Percival	Anthony Gelling
Josh Jones	Dan Sarginson
Adam Swift	Joe Burgess
Mark Flanagan	Blake Green
Lance Hohaia	Matty Smith
Kyle Amor	Ben Flower
James Roby	Sam Powell
Mose Masoe	Dom Crosby
Louie McCarthy-Scarsbrook	Joel Tomkins
Sia Soliola	Liam Farrell
Jordan Turner	Sean O'Loughlin

Subs

Willie Manu	Eddy Pettybourne
Alex Walmsley	Tony Clubb
Greg Richards	John Bateman
Luke Thompson	George Williams

Coaches

Nathan Brown	Shaun Wane

Tries

Soliola	Burgess
Makinson	

Goals

Percival (3)	Smith (1)

Referee: Phil Bentham

Tommy Makinson is the second player in this book to select the 2014 Grand Final as their favourite game. It doesn't come as a shock because it was their first Grand Final success since beating Hull in 2006.

St Helens as a club had to endure five successive Grand Final defeats before finally getting that monkey off their back with the win over Wigan.

Every St Helens player will tell you that beating Wigan at any time is special, but to do it on the grand stage at Old Trafford will take some beating.

Aside from recalling the moment he scored the winning try, Makinson reveals that he almost gave the game away because of injury. He admits to being in a bad place and felt he couldn't get back to full fitness.

He pays tribute to his parents and partner for their love and encouragement that helped him kick on and get his career back on track. He admits that every success he has ever had in the game, and any more in the future, will be dedicated to those closest to him.

I don't think my game will be a shock to anyone reading this to be honest. It was the first bit of silverware I ever won in my career, well the first main bit of silverware and that was the 2014 Grand Final.

I think we were written off pretty early against a great Wigan side and obviously they went a man down and from then on my dreams unfolded in front of me. I've got that dream of scoring a late try and helping us win the trophy, that's something that will live with me for ever. After being a fan for so long, coming to Old Trafford and watching the lads – Old Trafford is my favourite place in the world, so actually getting to set foot on that pitch and live my dreams, that's the greatest game I have ever played in by far.

It was a strange start, obviously with Ben Flower getting sent off and us losing Lance Hohaia. Everyone expected us to coast through them with 12 men, but Wigan just seemed to get better. They obviously didn't play to their full potential, but Wigan just upped their game and it was hard. They took the lead in the first half with Joe Burgess scoring a try before the break. We seemed to let our game slide and went away from a few of things we were doing well. During that season, we weren't a team that slung the ball around a lot. We just ground it down and played simple, basic rugby and when it came to the business end, we got over the line.

That game, we started to throw some passes out that were never on and put a few kicks in. We had forwards playing in the halves, full-backs playing at loose forward, wingers playing at full-back, it was crazy and it was mad for about 50 minutes. It was only the last sort of 25 minutes that we settled down and got into our groove and it is the last 20 minutes or so that we were remembered for.

The 80 minutes was amazing, but the hour or two after winning the Grand Final is kind of surreal. It was frightening, my thoughts went back to being that kid who was sat at Old Trafford with his dad. We used to go on the tram every year to watch Wigan or Saints play in a Grand Final, and then actually being the guy standing up with the Super League trophy in his arms looking at his mum and dad in the crowd ... that was my dream as a player. It was just everything I ever wanted, all I ever wanted to do when I played rugby was not to win the Golden Boot, not win the Man of Steel, not be in the Dream Team, it was to just lift the trophy with my team-mates. It's a team sport that we play, it's not about individual honours. My dream when I started off was to first win the Challenge Cup and then the Grand Final, those two trophies were just high on my list of things I wanted to do.

Going back to the game, I don't really remember much about the try I scored. I just remember running down the short side and seeing Wello [Paul Wellens] there, Jordan Turner was on the left side and it looked like the ball was going to go in that direction. I was like, please don't pass it to the left, Wello put a kick inside for me. I was just calling for him to do it, and he's shouting back, 'I'm putting it in, I'm putting it in.' I didn't know if the kick was going to be on the floor, or whether it was going to be high. I was just thinking, I'll follow the play and chase it and we'll see what happens. The rest is history really, I just remember jumping up, coming down with it. It was literally like it was in slow motion, it's mad the way things turn up. It went so slow and I just remember seeing the ball down and thinking, am I in here, have I grounded it properly? Then after that it was pure joy and elation. It was magic.

We knew Wigan would throw everything at us as they had to chase the game, I remember making a few good tackles. I was hardly in the game attacking really, it's strange because I had really worked on my attacking game as I love attacking. But in that Grand Final I was hardly in the game. I was just called on mainly in defence and that last ten minutes was mental. I was just throwing myself at everyone, I remember tackling Liam Farrell, Josh Charnley, George Williams, all of them. It was unreal, nothing was getting past me. I honestly did think they were going to score because they were throwing everything at us. I kept looking at the clock, we kicked it to the sideline, we were eight points up with one minute and ten seconds left, I was like this could be it here. I still get goosebumps thinking about it now, it's magic.

I remember seeing Wello on his knees, I think that picture will be remembered forever. Especially with Wello as captain; he's won everything there is to win in the game and him being captain and thinking his career is coming to an end, it was just special. I think Wello knew his time was coming to an end, injuries were catching up with him. His hip was playing up, his knee was playing up. How much Wello has done in his career and how good a player he had been, how he led us that year, it was just extra special for him. I just always remember watching him lift that trophy and the speech he made, he is just pure class in every sense. I just remember the speech, he thanked everyone and then he picked that trophy up and never looked back. He was the coolest guy in the stadium, he said a few words and when he picked it up, I was just bursting with pride. Looking at my family and friends and the supporters who had followed us all year, it burns me inside to do that again, because it is a feeling, I imagine, if you do it again it will never get worse. It always seems to get better, so let's hope we can do it again.*

How did it all begin? I was playing my rugby at Hindley to start with when I was younger, then I moved to St Jude's and that's where my career started going on the up. I played a few games and Mike Rush spotted me playing for St Jude's against Leigh Easts, or something like that. They approached me and wanted to invite me to the foundation squad as it was known back then. It went from there really, I went to Australia and toured there with Saints and played really well. After that, they offered me a full-time deal and I made my first-team debut in 2011. I played my first Grand Final in that year as well, but sadly we lost that one.

It's not been plain sailing throughout my career, I have had some bad injuries. Injuries can define you in different ways. I have kicked on from each injury I have had. I would read books about the likes of Tom Brady and other famous athletes, different people who play different sports and injuries can have a bad outcome where they can finish you off, or they can inspire you to kick on. The minute I got my second bad injury – I did my ankle then I did my cruciate ligament which is a common injury nowadays – I was thinking bad things and not sure what I was going to do. I didn't know whether I would pack the sport in, because it wasn't just on me. It was on my family as well, they felt the pain too, you would go home every day in a bad mood. People think about rugby league being a great sport, but there are definitely highs and lows. It's just like any other job in that sense. I was in a bad place, but I got back on the horse and I was helped by people at the club, new coaches, physios and more importantly my family. My family helped me get back to where I belonged, I just trained my absolute arse off to be fair to get to where I am today and that will never stop.

The days like winning the Grand Final and winning the Golden Boot, they are obviously good for me, but they mean a lot to my mum and dad, my partner and my kids. My kids are only young, and having to look at what their mum was going through when I was coming home in a bad mood every single day, not wanting to do anything or go out, everything I achieve now is for them. I look where I have come and every day I had my missus or mum and dad telling me 'you can do this, you can come back from any injury, you are one of the best players'. I was just thinking, no I can't. But they got me through it and all my success is me saying thank you to them, and how much their hard work means to me, along with my coaches and team-mates around me.

Since this interview, St Helens and Tommy Makinson have won the Grand Final again when they defeated Salford Red Devils in 2019.

JAMES ROBY

James Roby

HOOKER 2004–present
HERITAGE NUMBER 1136

BORN: 22 November 1985, St Helens

SIGNED: Date unknown from Blackbrook

DEBUT: 19 March 2004 vs Widnes Vikings

LAST GAME: N/A

ST HELENS CAREER: 454 appearances (including 138 as a substitute), 107 tries, 1 goal, 1 drop goal

HONOURS: Challenge Cup 2006, 2007, 2008; Super League 2006, 2014, 2019; World Club Challenge 2007; League Leaders' Shield 2005, 2006, 2007, 2008, 2014, 2018, 2019; Man of Steel 2007

LEFT: Still at the club

PLAYING CAREER: St Helens (2004–present)

James Roby seems to have been at St Helens for ever. It's very difficult to remember a time when he wasn't in the first team and causing all teams a whole host of problems with his darts from dummy half.

He joined the club from amateur side Blackbrook and played for the Under 19s and a handful of games with the

Under 21s, before Ian Millward gave him the chance he had dreamed of – playing in the first team at St Helens.

After a couple of games, and a spell out of the team, Roby was back in contention and he has been a first team member ever since. He spent the early part of his career playing as back-up hooker to Keiron Cunningham, but during 2007 his performances off the bench in a year that saw the Saints win the Challenge Cup, League Leaders' Shield and the World Club Challenge, earned him the Man of Steel award as the best player of the season.

It is a game from that season that Roby has decided to focus on. As he admits, when you have played over 450 games for one club it is very difficult just to pinpoint one game. After a lot of thinking, he opted to choose the 2007 Challenge Cup Final against Catalans Dragons – the first one at the new Wembley Stadium.

Roby goes on to explain what it is like to play at a stadium like Wembley, and how he tried to block out the outside world and just prepare naturally for a game.

Since making his debut in 2004, Roby has always been linked with a move away from St Helens – especially to the NRL in Australia. Roby likes to think he is an honest and loyal person and admits he feels very privileged to have played for his home-town club for so long, something he wouldn't change for the world.

St Helens 30-8 Catalans Dragons
Challenge Cup Final
Saturday, 25 August 2007
Wembley Stadium, London
Attendance 84,241

Teams
St Helens   *Catalans Dragons*
Paul Wellens   Clint Greenshields
Ade Gardner   Justin Murphy
Matt Gidley   John Wilson
Willie Talau   Sebastien Raguin
Francis Meli   Younes Khattabi
Leon Pryce   Adam Mogg
Sean Long   Stacey Jones
Nick Fozzard   Jerome Guisset
Keiron Cunningham   Luke Quigley
Jason Cayless   Alex Chan
Lee Gilmour   Jason Croker
Mike Bennett   Cyrille Gossard
Jon Wilkin   Gregory Mounis

Subs
James Roby   Remi Casty
James Graham   David Ferriol
Paul Clough   Vincent Duport
Maurie Fa'asavalu   Kane Bentley

Coaches
Daniel Anderson   Mick Potter

Tries
Roby   Khattabi
Gardner (2)   Murphy
Wellens
Clough

Goals
Long (5)

Referee: Ashley Klein

In 1999, the last Challenge Cup to be played under the Twin Towers of Wembley Stadium took place between Leeds Rhinos and London Broncos. Seven Challenge Cup Finals were contested in different parts of the UK before the new Wembley was finally ready to host a rugby league game.

That rugby league game was the 2007 Challenge Cup Final on Saturday, 25 August and it saw St Helens go up against rank outsiders Catalans Dragons in the blazing heat.

To play at Wembley at any time must be a special feeling, but Roby takes immense pride in being the first rugby league player to score a try at the new stadium. That try opened the scoring that day and helped Saints go on to record a 30-8 success to see them lift the famous trophy for the second year in succession. They had beaten Huddersfield Giants 42-12 at Twickenham Stadium in 2006.

The game was deadlocked at 0-0 when Roby entered the fray. He then settled everyone's nerves as he broke through to score the opening try. That most certainly settled the fans down, and St Helens eventually ran out comfortable winners with Ade Gardner helping himself to two tries, while Paul Wellens and Paul Clough also got on the score sheet.

The Lance Todd Trophy award for man of the match in the Challenge Cup Final was shared between two players for only the second time in the history of the competition as Leon Pryce and Paul Wellens both got the same number of votes from the members of the press.

Roby is not a player you would ever say was arrogant and big-headed, but he admitted it was difficult picking *one game ahead of all the others because he was fortunate enough to play in an era that saw the Saints lift a staggering 15 pieces of silverware – and at time of writing that figure was not finished.*

He has loved his time at St Helens, but there was a time when he thought his chance had gone begging. He missed out on a scholarship and thought he would be discarded, but he worked hard and was determined to prove his doubters wrong. He certainly has done that, as he will go down as one of the greatest players ever to play for St Helens.

The best game I've ever played in? It's a difficult question to be honest, it's taking me a while to come up with just one.

Early on in my career I remember playing a few games at the DW Stadium against Wigan and as a young lad still making his way in the team if you like, those occasions were massive. They were normally sold out on Good Friday and all that kind of stuff, it was great. But I suppose when you have to pin one game down as the match of my life, I would have to say all the finals stick in the memory so I will probably say the Challenge Cup Final in 2007.

I was lucky enough to come on from the bench and score the first try at the new Wembley. It was against Catalans Dragons and we were kind of expected to win if you like, but Catalans were a great team. I think there was a little bit of pressure on us as everyone thought we would win easily. But when I think back to 2005, 2006, 2007 and even 2008 – that era we had a team full of superstars and I was still very much one of the young lads and a bench player. I remember the game was very tit for tat, it was 0-0 and I came on. It is very rare that a game is 0-0 after half an hour, I remember I came on and I immediately made an impact by going through, beating a couple of defenders and going over for the try.

To score a try at Wembley, in front of your own fans was fantastic, you will never forget that kind of moment. We went on to win the game and I just remember being so happy that we had won. It was a privilege to be the first team to play and lift a trophy at the new Wembley, everyone was excited about being at the new Wembley. The year before we had played at Twickenham in the Challenge Cup Final while Wembley was obviously getting finished; to go there and play was absolutely fantastic. I remember everything just seemed on a bigger scale at Wembley; the changing rooms are huge, you have a warm-up area and the benches in the room are better than the benches anywhere else. The tunnel is even bigger, you go out into the stadium and it is ridiculous. It is so big, and it makes playing at your home ground seem pretty small. You look up and it is three tiers. It is just huge.

The beauty of it is, you get to go there during the week and even train there the day before the game. It is empty, but you get to kind of experience it and almost get those nerves out of the way a little bit in terms of preparation. It really helps, so when you go out on game day it is not brand new. It familiarises you with the surroundings a little bit, it makes you a bit more at ease. Especially on a game day, you are prepared and you are ready. I try to simplify it; as long as everything is going to plan and in place, I am happy. I don't want any hassle on game day. I know a lot of lads are superstitious and they have this and that, but I just want to be ready and prepared and there is nothing more I can do, so don't worry about it. As long as I am comfortable in my surroundings and all that kind of stuff, it kind of makes game day stress-free. So, going there the day before probably just chills you out a little bit more, so when you do get there you know exactly where you are going and you know what the changing rooms look like, you know your route to the pitch and where the warm-up room is.

Saying that though, nothing can ever hit you like when you go out for the warm-up or for kick-off, the hairs on the back of your neck stand up and the noise and everything hits you. Then again, I've been lucky enough to play in quite a few big games over the years, so my advice would be to take it in. Get it all in before the kick-off, don't take 10 or 20 minutes into the game to realise where you are. It's only another game at the end of the day, you just want to play the same kind of rugby you have been playing everywhere else, it is just that your surroundings are different. I always tried to look around during the warm-up and take everything in, experience the whole atmosphere because once kick-off arrived, I would forget all that and focus on the match.

It is nice to look back on your career. I am obviously a St Helens lad and I was playing at Blackbrook amateur club for my whole amateur career, I started when I was about seven. It was a bit different to what they do now. Now they don't start looking at kids until they are about 14-ish, and nowadays they don't have a Town team or North West Counties but when I was a kid from under 11s onwards, we had a St Helens Town team and we were always playing against the likes of Warrington and Wigan. I was lucky enough to represent the Town and as we got older, we had Lancashire teams and North West Counties collective and I played in them. I used to get invited to come and train with Saints as a junior from being 13 years of age and I did that for a few years. I carried on playing amateur and I just progressed and got to the age where clubs give out scholarships. I remember I never actually got a scholarship, and quite a few of my mates did. I was gutted and maybe, without realising it at the time, that was probably one of the best things that ever happened to me because it probably spurred me on and made me more determined to succeed and think 'hang on, I want what they have. I think I'm pretty good'.

I thought I was a good amateur and I was good enough to be in the representative teams and then in my late teens I was probably just outside the core group at St Helens in terms of the kids coming through. Some people might have thought 'I don't know about him'. So, that made me fight hard to prove my worth and I remember having a good year with the Saints Under 19s and I was 17 at the time. I had a really good year and they promoted me to the Under 21s. We started the season, and I had only played a handful of games and we were training on the front of Knowsley Road and Ian Millward came over after training one day and said, 'I've watched a few games and I think you are going well.' This was on a Monday or Tuesday night and he said, 'I want you to come training on Wednesday with the first team.' I was bricking it to be honest with you, I went training with them for one day and he said, 'You are on the bench on Friday.'

Nowadays, lads normally get promoted to the first team and then they have to train for a couple of years in that environment on a day-to-day basis as a professional before they get their chance. I was like fast-tracked and it happened a bit quick. I made my debut three days later after my first training session. I stayed in and around the team for a couple of months, but never played again. But then, midway through that season, I was brought in again, and I played every game to the end. I probably didn't do it the traditional way in terms of working my way through every system. I went from the 19s to a couple of games for the 21s and then straight into the first team.

My heart will always be here. I am a St Helens lad and home grown and I'm very proud to be the captain of St Helens. I know how privileged I am, especially to come through when I did with the team we had and to play in that successful era when we were winning loads of trophies. I have had a great career and I am thankful to St Helens for looking after me and I have managed to make a living out of it for 15 years. My heart is St Helens and I would like to think I am a loyal person and quite an honest person. I am pretty laid back and I find it very easy to switch off from my rugby. I'm happy where I am to be honest.

LOUIE McCARTHY-SCARSBROOK

Louie McCarthy-Scarsbrook

PROP FORWARD/LOOSE FORWARD 2010 –Present
HERITAGE NUMBER 1186

BORN: 14 January 1986, Whitechapel, London

SIGNED: 3 September 2010 from Harlequins RL

DEBUT: 12 February 2011 vs Wigan Warriors

LAST GAME: N/A

ST HELENS CAREER: 281 appearances (including 140 as a substitute), 57 tries (at the time of writing)

HONOURS: Super League 2014, 2019; League Leaders' Shield 2014, 2018, 2019

LEFT: Still at the club

PLAYING CAREER: Harlequins RL (2006–10), St Helens (2011–present day)

Louie McCarthy-Scarsbrook is a rare breed – a southerner at the top of his game in rugby league is not something you see every day. Yes, there are a few people from down south who have made it big, but LMS has been at the top of his game for the past ten years.

St Helens took a punt on LMS back in 2011 when they lured him away from Harlequins RL to move from London to the north-west of England. No one would have batted an eyelid

195

if he had gone back south a year or two later, complaining of being homesick.

He didn't do that, he stuck to his guns and carved out a great career with the Saints. In his own words, he is now part of the furniture.

LMS is one of the players every opposing fan loves to hate. He seems to get under everyone's skin and that's what makes the Saints fans love him so much. During his time at Saints, he has won two Grand Finals and he is hungry to win a few more.

In this chapter, LMS talks about the 2019 Grand Final triumph and how he did an impression of a famous former Australian tennis player after Saints had beaten Salford. He also reveals why it was a no-brainer that his testimonial game for St Helens in 2020 was against London Broncos.

St Helens 23-6 Salford Red Devils
2019 Super League Grand Final
Saturday, 12 October 2019
Old Trafford, Manchester
Attendance 64,102

Teams

St Helens	*Salford Red Devils*
Lachlan Coote	Niall Evalds
Tommy Makinson	Ken Sio
Kevin Naiqama	Kris Welham
Mark Percival	Jake Bibby
Regan Grace	Krisnan Inu
Theo Fages	Tui Lolohea
Jonny Lomax	Jackson Hastings
Alex Walmsley	Lee Mossop
James Roby	Logan Tomkins
Luke Thompson	Gil Dudson
Zeb Taia	Josh Jones
Dominique Peyroux	George Griffin
Morgan Knowles	Tyrone McCarthy

Subs

Louie McCarthy-Scarsbrook	Joey Lussick
Kyle Amor	Mark Flanagan
Jack Ashworth	Adam Walker
Aaron Smith	Greg Burke

Coaches

Justin Holbrook	Ian Watson

Tries

Knowles	Bibby
Tai	
Percival	

Goals

Coote (5)	Inu

Drop Goals
Makinson

Referee: Chris Kendall

Louie McCarthy-Scarsbrook has been lucky enough to have appeared in three Grand Finals at Old Trafford during his time at St Helens, but it is their 2019 victory there that makes LMS most proud.

In that year, St Helens were head and shoulders better than everyone else in Super League. They won the League Leaders' Shield with ease and ended up a staggering 16 points clear of their nearest rivals Wigan Warriors in second place.

Justin Holbrook's men only lost three times in the league all season, booking their place in the Grand Final with another convincing win over Wigan. The Red Vee ran in seven tries with Mark Percival scoring twice, while Kevin Naiqama, Jonny Lomax, Theo Fages, Luke Thompson and Zeb Taia all crossed as they hammered their most hated rivals 40-10.

That win over Wigan allowed them to have a week off as they prepared for the Grand Final. Everyone just expected their opponents to be Wigan as they were going up against Salford for the second time in three weeks. Wigan won the first encounter 18-12 in round one of the play-offs, but the Red Devils got some revenge in week three as they won 28-4 to set up a Grand Final meeting with the Saints.

Salford deserved their place in the Grand Final, but they were no real match for the Saints at Old Trafford as Holbrook's men ran out 23-6 winners with Morgan Knowles, Zeb Taia and Mark Percival putting the icing on a very sweet season.

When I first signed for Saints, I never thought I'd be here long enough to have a testimonial. I actually thought it was just by accident that they wanted me, so I went along with it. But now I have been here for ten years, it's really special and I must have pulled some wool over people's eyes. They can't get rid of me now; I am part of the furniture.

When I was told I was having a testimonial game, it was always my choice that the game would be against London Broncos. They were my first team. I have only had two clubs and it just seemed right. I wanted them because Dave Hughes is still there and Wardy [Danny Ward] the head coach, who I played with, so it was a no-brainer. I played at the club under different circumstances, but the owner is still there, and I had a great relationship with him, so it just made sense.

My best game for Saints? Now you are asking, my memory isn't the greatest. You know what, I know a lot of people will probably say the same thing, but it would have to be the Grand Final in 2019 against Salford Red Devils. I think Salford played really well in that game at Old Trafford, but we played better and it was a great team performance. To top it off how we did was just great, we were just solid. I wouldn't say anyone was electric, but everyone did their job and that's how you win Grand Finals.

Leading up to the game, we knew everyone was backing us and you have asked the question that everyone does: 'How do you keep grounded?' Well, for me that is easy. I just don't read anything about rugby league. It's perfect, just read absolutely nothing. Don't look at anything, if anything just look at the pictures on Instagram. You don't have to read it then. I never really pay any attention to what is written in the papers, I'm more of a football fan away from the game really. So, my way of getting prepared for big games is to listen to or watch football; I can switch myself off from it. Some players can't and they live and breathe the game, but I do have an off switch. I rarely read stuff about rugby league, it's a good way to be because I can just go home and not worry about anything.

I remember everything about that game in 2019. I had been there before, and I cannot remember anything from the 2011 Grand Final. I remember everything from the 2014 win over Wigan and this one I can remember everything. In 2011, it went so quick and we lost and I was devastated so I wanted to forget about that forever. After that defeat by Leeds, I remember saying to myself to take it all in, take it all in. It was amazing.

What sticks in my mind the most was after the game, after we had won. My dad has got a bad back, so he is ruined and he was quite high up in the stands at Old Trafford. It was after all the celebrations had taken place and a lot of people had already gone, I climbed over and walked over to my old man and gave him a cuddle. That was special, it was a bit of a Pat Cash moment when he did it at the tennis at Wimbledon. I went up and gave him a cuddle and it was really nice. All my family were there around him, and with him being a big girl he was crying his eyes out. No tears from me, I had drunk too much champagne celebrating.

After the game we were all in the sheds, we ruined the Manchester United home sheds, there was champagne and beer everywhere. Everyone was just throwing it at each other for about a good three hours. Then we made our way back to the stadium at St Helens and we had a good celebration there. Some boys went into town and then we just got together the next day and the following day after that we all went to Dublin, so it was a good celebration. Enough said about that, ha ha!

What made us so good in 2019? We had good recruitment that year, we signed a good full-back. It is hard when you lose a player like Ben Barba, but Lachlan Coote came in and he steadied the ship and he was just a calm head at the back. He was one player who could guide us around the field, we also didn't get many big injuries during that season which is always good. When you don't get injuries, you can keep the same squad playing and build more consistency. The best thing we had during that season was consistency. We had good consistent performances for a good block of the season. If we can keep that up and play how we did in 2019 and work on the things we need to and improve in other areas, I can't see us going too far wrong in the next few years. Hopefully, we will improve.

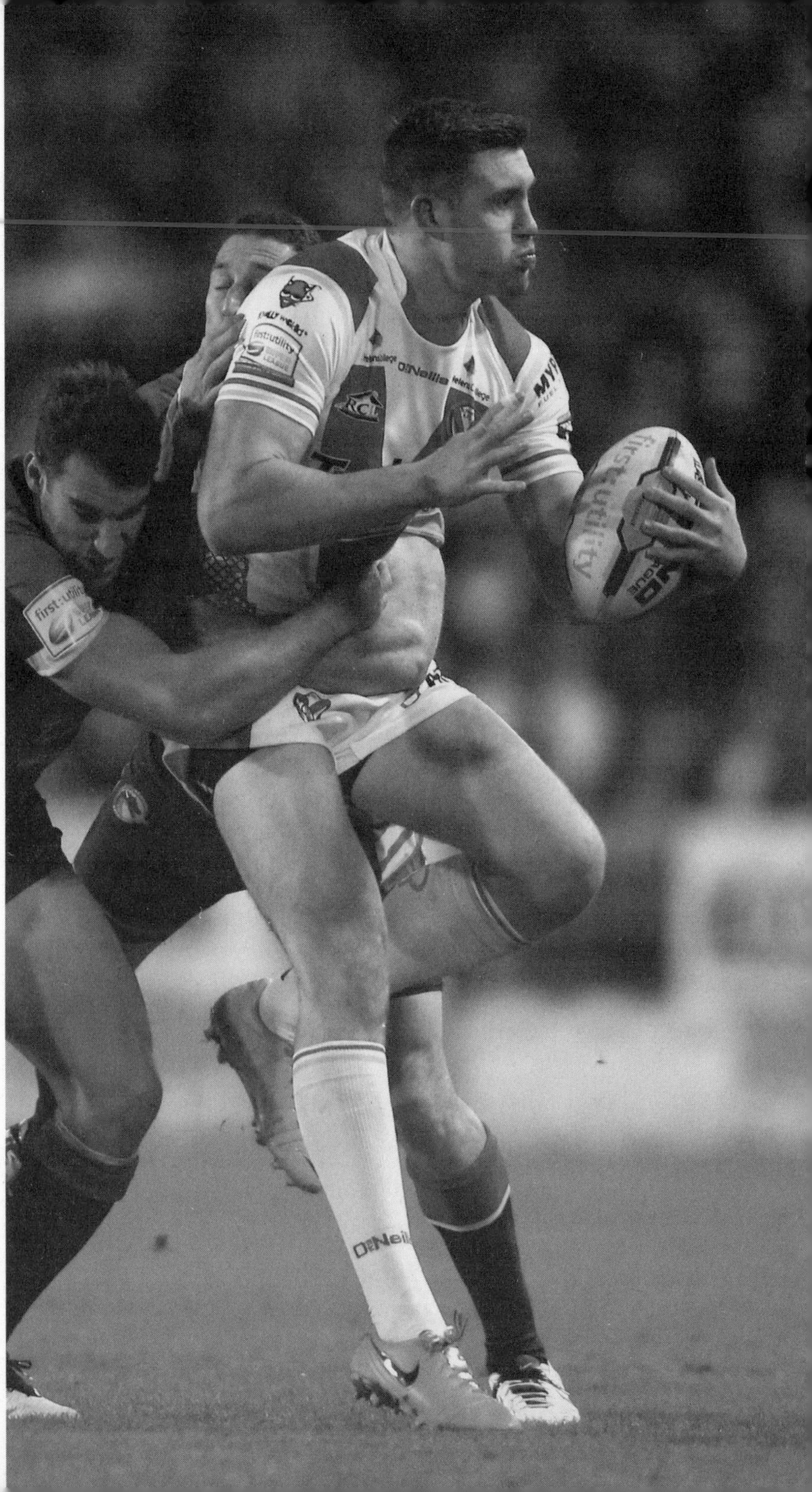

JOE GREENWOOD

Joe Greenwood

SECOND-ROW 2012–17
HERITAGE NUMBER 1198

BORN: 2 April 1993, Oldham, England

SIGNED: 2011 from Saddleworth Rangers

DEBUT: 27 April 2012 vs Oldham Roughyeds

LAST GAME: 9 February 2017 vs Leeds Rhinos

ST HELENS CAREER: 77 appearances (including 32 as a substitute), 26 tries

HONOURS: Super League 2014; League Leaders' Shield 2014

LEFT: 2017 to join Gold Coast Titans

PLAYING CAREER: St Helens (2012–17), Gold Coast Titans (2017–18), Wigan Warriors (2018–present)

Joe Greenwood might not be an obvious choice to be included in this book, but the fact is he enjoyed his time at St Helens and always gave his all.

He joined the club in 2011 from amateur side Saddleworth Rangers, and although he was named 18th man on a number of occasions, he would only make his first team debut in 2012.

His debut came in the fifth round of the Challenge Cup against his home club – Oldham – with the Saints running out 76-0 winners. Greenwood came off the bench in that game as Francis Meli scored a hat-trick of tries with Josh Jones and Jonny Lomax grabbing two apiece.

His Super League debut came a week later in a 38-12 win over Wakefield Trinity, as he once again came off the bench. His only other appearance in Super League that season was a 26-18 away win at Wigan in September.

It was in 2013 that he really started to get noticed; he made 14 appearances that season and scored three tries. His most prolific season as a try-scoring forward came in 2016 when he crossed for 11 tries in 24 appearances before he made his move to the Gold Coast Titans in February 2017.

St Helens 0-39 South Sydney Rabbitohs
World Club Challenge
Sunday, 22 February 2015
Langtree Park, St Helens
Attendance 17,980

Teams

St Helens	*South Sydney Rabbitohs*
Jonny Lomax	Greg Inglis
Tommy Makinson	Alex Johnston
Mark Percival	Dylan Walker
Jordan Turner	Bryson Goodwin
Adam Swift	Joel Reddy
Travis Burns	Luke Keary
Jon Wilkin	Adam Reynolds
Kyle Amor	George Burgess
James Roby	Issac Luke
Mose Masoe	David Tyrrell
Joe Greenwood	Glenn Stewart
Atelea Vea	John Sutton
Mark Flanagan	Ben Lowe

Subs

Louie McCarthy-Scarsbrook	Chris McQueen
Alex Walmsley	Thomas Burgess
Andre Savelio	Chris Grevsmuhl
Luke Thompson	Jason Clark

Coaches

Keiron Cunningham	Michael Maguire

Tries
Reddy 2, Stewart
Walker, Inglis
Keary, McQueen

Goals
Reynolds (5)
Drop Goal
Reynolds

Referee: Richard Silverwood

Joe Greenwood is the only player in this whole book who actually chose a defeat as his favourite ever game in a Saints shirt – but it's not that difficult to understand why.

The game he has chosen is the 2015 World Club Challenge against South Sydney Rabbitohs at Langtree Park with both teams playing to see who would be crowned the best rugby league team in the world.

The Saints set up this tie thanks to a narrow 14-6 win over 12-man Wigan Warriors in the Super League Grand Final at Old Trafford, while the Bunnies won the NRL Grand Final with a convincing 30-6 victory over Canterbury Bulldogs in a game that will be remembered for Sam Burgess playing nearly 80 minutes with a broken cheekbone following a clash of heads with James Graham.

Greenwood was not part of the 17-man squad that defeated the Warriors in the Grand Final, but he was named in the second row to face Souths in the World Club Challenge in what was arguably Greenwood's biggest game to date.

The Saints failed to score that day as the Bunnies won 39-0 with Joel Reddy scoring two tries, while Glenn Stewart, Dylan Walker, Greg Inglis, Luke Keary and Chris McQueen all crossed over.

Greenwood believes because of who the opposition were that day, he grew up as a player and it stood him in good stead when he eventually moved out to Australia with the Gold Coast Titans.

During this chapter, Greenwood reveals the main reason why he joined Wigan and what the reaction was when the story broke, plus he also talks about the head injuries that looked to derail his career in 2019.

I think the game that sticks out the most during my time at Saints as my biggest game would have to be the World Club Challenge in 2015 against the South Sydney Rabbitohs. I know we ended up losing heavily, but I was up against the Burgess boys – George and Thomas – Gregg Inglis, Adam Reynolds and John Sutton. Amazing players.

I was only 20 years old and I feel that game taught me a lot for the remainder of my career. Playing against players like that, you learn a lot from them. That was a massive game, the emotion was off the chart with the build-up to the game. It was a full house at Langtree Park, I remember walking out and looking over and you have got the Australian players all stood there and at 20 years old you think, wow, what is going on? You do really have to pinch yourself.

To me it was a life lesson as well, not just a game of rugby league. Some of their contacts and collisions were quite ferocious, but you have to be a man about it. We ended up getting beat quite convincingly, but I felt like I held my head high and gave a good account of myself. I just did what I could to be honest, I think a lot of other players did the same.

For me, playing against the Souths in that game has helped me a lot in my career. I'm not sure if that was the game that made Gold Coast Titans come in for me, I was just trying to be the best person and player I could be at the time. My aim every week was to beat my opposite number – it still is to be honest with you – and then the move to Australia just fell into place. A couple of clubs were showing an interest and I ended up going over there, it was fast-tracked, and I loved every minute of it. Having already played against the Bunnies, I wanted more of it and also to see what life was like over in Australia.

The move to Gold Coast will never be a regret of mine, things happen for a reason. When the Titans came in and said they wanted me over in the NRL, I was buzzing because I wanted to see what that side of the world was like. Not just the playing rugby side of it, I wanted to embrace the lifestyle as well. I am so pleased to have been given the opportunity to go over to Australia and play in the NRL.

I don't think everyone was pleased that I chose to sign for Wigan rather than go back to St Helens. I have been told not to go around town or my kneecaps will get done and stuff like that. You just read messages like that and laugh it off, what else can you do? Wigan and Saints is a massive rivalry, it's like someone going to Manchester City from Manchester United in football: it's huge. Both sets of fans take pride in their home town. With me being out of the town, it was a good time to go to Wigan. They have a massive history. You have to do what is best for you in your career; the career of a rugby league player is so short and before you know it you blink and you are in your mid-thirties and you have to look for a new career. I can always look back when I retire on what I have done; hopefully there is a lot more years to come but I am happy with my career so far and the decisions I've made.

In recent years, I have picked up a few knocks – including some to the head. It was just a freakish thing [the head knocks], they have looked back on the video and they are just head collisions and that is what you get in rugby. I had three in 2019, I've had them in previous years but not as many as that in such a short space of time. I was a little bit worried at the start, but I've been back doing contact work in defence and everything looks fine going forward. You can't really give those past knocks much thought when you are playing, because if you hold back and go in half-hearted, then you are more than likely going to come out with an injury. You just put it to the back of your mind and get on with it, it's part and parcel of the game. You will get knocks here and there, unfortunately I ended up getting a few but hopefully I have had my fair share of knocks now and I can kick on with my career.

TOMMY FRODSHAM

Tommy Frodsham

STAND-OFF 1989–1990
HERITAGE NUMBER 1015

BORN: 12 January 1962, St Helens

SIGNED: 30 August 1989 from Swinton

DEBUT: 10 September 1989 vs Castleford Tigers

LAST GAME: 2 December 1990 vs Swinton

ST HELENS CAREER: 21 appearances, 8 tries

HONOURS: None

LEFT: 1990 to join Swinton

PLAYING CAREER: Blackpool (1985–87), Swinton (1987–89), St Helens (1989–90), Swinton (1991), Runcorn (1992)

Tommy Frodsham might not be the most famous player in this book, but he played the greatest sport on earth and therefore has every right to be able to tell his story.

He joined the Saints from Swinton in 1989 and went on to make 21 appearances for the club. He failed to win any silverware during his brief stint with the club, but he was part of the side that got all the way to the Challenge Cup semi-finals.

Frodsham joked that it wouldn't be too difficult to pick out his best game, seeing as there weren't many of them, but he has opted to choose their win away at Hull in the second round of the Challenge Cup, a game which was, in fact, Mike McClennan's first match in charge as head coach following the axing of Alex Murphy.

Frodsham retells the tale of how McClennan allowed the whole squad to go out around town in Hull the night before the game, and left it to their own judgement on how they behaved and whether or not they drank any alcohol.

As a player, Frodsham was a clever stand-off and could make his way through a gap in a blink of an eye. He wasn't as quick as he thought during that win at The Boulevard in 1990. Frodsham managed to score eight tries for St Helens in his spell, with two of them coming in the same game against Featherstone Rovers in only his second league start for the club.

Hull 12-24 St Helens
Challenge Cup Second Round
Saturday, 10 February 1990
The Boulevard, Hull
Attendance 8,066

Teams

Hull	*St Helens*
Richard Gay	Gary Connolly
Paul Eastwood	Alan Hunte
Brian Blacker	Phil Veivers
Marquis Charles	Paul Loughlin
Neil Turner	Les Quirk
Greg Mackey	Tommy Frodsham
Phil Windley	Sean Devine
Karl Harrison	Paul Forber
Lee Jackson	Paul Groves
Andy Dannatt	George Mann
Noel Cleal	Bernard Dwyer
Russ Walker	Roy Haggerty
Steve McNamara	Shane Cooper

Subs

Jon Sharp	Mark Bailey
Paul Welham	Chris Arkwright

Coaches

Brian Smith	Mike McClennan

Tries

Dannatt	Connolly
McNamara	Dwyer
	Haggerty
	Quirk
	Veivers

Goals

Eastwood (2)	Loughlin (2)

Referee: Gerry Kershaw

A lot of players who have been interviewed for this book have had the luxury of picking from a number of massive games or finals. Unfortunately that luxury is not afforded to Tommy Frodsham.

Frodsham only played 21 times for the Saints, and the biggest game of his Saints career was the 1990 Challenge Cup semi-final against Wigan at Old Trafford.

That is not the game Frodsham has chosen, because it ended in defeat. So, he has opted to go for an earlier game in that Challenge Cup run when they travelled to take on Hull FC at The Boulevard.

Frodsham has chosen this particular game because it is one that every Saints fan he comes into contact with seems to remember. There is one particular incident in the game which he can laugh about now, but at the time it could have cost St Helens the game.

Thankfully for Frodsham, Saints didn't buckle under pressure and they recorded a 24–12 win to set up a quarter-final tie against Whitehaven.

Frodsham reveals in this chapter how he ended up joining the Saints, and when he realised his days were numbered at the club.

The former stand-off is not bitter about the way his time at Saints came to an end; he admits he didn't have the dedication needed to play as a professional after a number of injury setbacks. After finally agreeing a release from Saints, he went on to play amateur rugby into his forties.

Thank you for involving me in this project, it is an absolute pleasure to share my memories of my time at St Helens. I didn't play many games for Saints. That was for many reasons – many will say because I just wasn't good enough, ha ha! So, to be asked for my most memorable is an honour.

I am selecting the last 16 of the Silk Cut Challenge Cup, which was a televised tie on the BBC when we took on Hull FC at The Boulevard in 1990. It's memorable for lots of reasons.

I had been out injured for a while, following broken ribs in the Regal Trophy semi-final defeat against Halifax. That was a very painful day: not only was I in agony with the injury, we also lost the game 10-9 at Central Park and missed out on the chance of taking on Wigan in the Regal Trophy Final.

I picked up the injury on 23 December, but played with this injury against Wigan on Boxing Day under anaesthetic and I played again with the pain in the January loss to Leigh away, which turned out to be Alex Murphy's last game in charge. I never did myself any favours. After that I decided to rest it until I was fully fit.

During this time Saints went on a cup run with Shane Cooper in temporary charge until Mike McClennan arrived. The Hull game in the Challenge Cup was Mike's first game in charge and my return to the first team, partnering Sean Devine at half-back.

Mike insisted on all the players staying in Beverley overnight prior to the game as some kind of team-building ritual, which was really, really unusual and still is to be honest. So, we prepared all week then headed for Hull on Friday morning, stopping off for a disastrous training session along the way.

Mike straight away demonstrated his unusual ways by allowing the whole team to go out on the town, the night before the game. That is definitely not something that would be allowed or tolerated in today's game. Obviously, there were caveats. He was trusting everyone to be sensible or abstain from alcohol altogether, and he called a team meeting at 11pm that night to make sure everyone got back.

You can imagine the reaction around Hull city centre, when the whole Saints team were out the night before an important match. However, I am very pleased to report that everyone was sensible (even Roy Haggerty) and the whole night went according to plan.

On this trip I became a lot closer to Saints team-mate and second-row forward Bernard Dwyer. I am actually still very close friends with Bernard to this day and he is godparent to my son Tomas along with his wife Jackie. I put him in for a try that day.

The game itself started as a very tense affair. We were in front narrowly at half-time with the scoreline 6-8. It was a very close game all the way through to be honest, but heading into the final quarter of the match, we showed our dominance and we started to pull away.

Their danger man was definitely Noel 'Crusher' Cleal, who we managed to keep quiet. We had to do our homework on players like that. He was a former Australia international and New South Wales State of Origin star, so he was a very good player, but we didn't allow him to get his own way. I can still remember them attacking our line and I flew out to try to shoulder-charge him and bounced away. It was like running into a brick wall, and he probably thought a fly had attacked him.

In the end we scored five tries to two to win the game 12-24 to set up a quarter-final tie away at Whitehaven, which we won 44-10 to set up a semi-final tie with Wigan at Old Trafford. We really thought we could go all the way to Wembley that year, but a late try from Andy Goodway for Wigan saw that dream come to an end.

Getting back to the game against Hull in the second round of the Challenge Cup, why it's memorable for me is because of an incident which should have been a moment of glory, but ended up nearly being disastrous. It's something ardent Saints fans regularly pull me up on. All I can say is that it's a good job we won.

At the start of the second half in our own 25, I took a short ball from George Mann which put me clean through, with only the full-back Richard Gay to beat. I had Lockers [Paul Loughlin] and Les Quirk to my left.

The obvious thing to do was just to draw the full-back and pass to Lockers, him to Quirky. Try and game over. However, I knew better.

I was always confident of sidestepping a full-back, I also wasn't great at passing right to left quickly. So, in my wisdom I thought I would sidestep the full-back, then give to Lockers. The first part went quite well, then I tried to get the pass in, but the centre had got himself in between us blocking the pass. I showed it and thought about getting it around him, but decided it now wasn't possible. So, I pinned my ears back and decided to go the remaining 50 yards for what would have been a spectacular try.

What I didn't plan for was on the opposite wing, in my way was Great Britain winger Paul Eastwood who hauled me down inches from the line. I can still hear Ray French now. 'Oh what has he done! Why didn't he pass?' That would have put the game to bed, I think we were leading 14-6 at the time, that would have put us out of sight. But we continued to fight hard and eventually came good. It shows the passion of the fans who can remember a moment like that which eventually did not actually make a difference to the result.

As I said, thank God we went on to win or I would have never lived it down. However, in the long run, maybe the coach formed an opinion of me that lasted. I do actually have the game on DVD somewhere.

I had a lot of bad injuries when I was younger, so all my friends signed [for professional clubs] but I kind of just lost my way. I had to do it the hard way in the end. I ended up at Thatto Heath under Frankie Barrow and he ended up being my mentor. I had trials with Warrington, I should have signed for Warrington actually before that. I actually had trials at a few clubs but the people who were advising me kept telling me they weren't offering enough money. Whenever an offer was made, they would go, 'It's not enough, hang on for more.' So, you would hang on for more and they just didn't come back. So, Warrington never came back for me. That was going on and Blackpool came along and I trialled with them and went straight into the first team, whereas with the other teams I would have been in the A team first.

I made my debut for Blackpool against Wakefield and I equalled their most tries in a match record while on trial with four tries. I did that twice actually. The record had been held since 1972 or something like that and I broke it on trial, they then signed me and I did it again the season after. I loved it at Blackpool, it was a great place to be at. I was there three seasons, then they became Springfield Borough, that was the beginning of the end really. I went to Springfield [in 1987], but it was the year that contracts came out, because in those days you signed for life. If you signed for a club, then that was it. You didn't get any extra money unless you were good enough to go and say you wanted more money, or you were leaving. When you used to get players staying away from clubs, it was because they were saying things like, 'Give me a grand, if you don't give me a grand then I won't play.' But in general, once you signed that was it. I signed for Springfield Borough on a contract where they paid you half up front. I was the worst negotiator with money there has ever been when I was playing. The other half of the contract was due at Christmas. When it came around to Christmas, they couldn't afford the other half, and if they don't pay you, you were a free agent. They swapped me for Danny Wilson – Ryan Giggs' dad – in a deal with Swinton, so I went to Swinton and they were in the first division back then.

I did a few seasons there, Peter Smethurst was coach and Frankie Barrow was there, and then I went to Australia in the off-season and played over there. When I got back to Swinton they had changed coaches with Jim Crellin becoming the head coach and he particularly didn't like me. So, I was dropped to the A team and I played in, coincidently, Tommy Martyn's first ever game for Oldham A team against Swinton, and I marked him. I put in a transfer request and they listed me at £100,000, I couldn't believe it. But they ended up doing a swap deal with Darren Bloor, so I basically hung around for a couple of weeks and then the swap deal came around and Darren Bloor went to Swinton and I went to Saints.

I should have made my debut against Sheffield Eagles away, but I was ill. I ended up playing the week later against Castleford. Murph [Alex Murphy] was the coach. I was never not picked that season, so in the 1989–90 season if ever I didn't play it was because I was injured. I didn't have much luck with injuries and then once Mike McClennan came in in place of Murph, really that was it for me, I think.

I got injured and I couldn't really come back from injury. I got injured again and again, and I was getting older. We had a tough cup run that year and we got to the semi-final, but when Murph got sacked they appointed Mike McClennan, but he couldn't come over straight away. So, Shane Cooper was appointed temporary coach and I was injured for all of that period, so any games that Mike would have watched before coming over I wouldn't have been in them. So, in his head, I was not the first-choice stand-off, although my first game back from injury was under him. I was back in straight away and he never didn't pick me until right until the end of the season, but [by then] I was injured anyway. He was a superstitious coach, so I think because we were on a cup run, he didn't change the team, but as soon as we got beat, I was out. Then I just couldn't come back, I had a shoulder injury and it just kept going on and on.

I had a big operation at the time. I went back to Swinton on loan on the basis that when the season was over they would operate on my shoulder, so I finished the season off in 1991 and that was the year Saints went to bloody Wembley. I wouldn't have played, but I would have been in the squad though. So, I missed out on a Wembley trip and as hard as I tried, I just couldn't come back from injury. Every time I tried to come back, I just got injured again and I couldn't get fit so that was it. That was me pretty much finished then.

Going back to the contract side of things, back then, as long as they offered you playing terms then that was deemed you had a contract offer, meaning I was stuck at Saints. All they had to do was offer me £50 a match or whatever, that was all I was on then. I couldn't go anywhere or play for anyone else. I couldn't even play amateur rugby. I couldn't do anything except play for Saints. I did go back and play in the A team, I enjoyed it in the A team, as I knew a lot of the young lads.

I played there for a bit longer until about 1992, I just packed in then and went back playing amateur rugby. I got a release from Saints in the end; they had to release you. They put me on the transfer list at first for like £25,000 and no one was going to pay that. I did about a year at the club where I couldn't do anything at all. I actually played four games at Runcorn for nothing because they couldn't afford to pay me because Saints were charging them for me playing there. They couldn't afford both, so I said I'll just play for nothing. Then I just finished, as I pestered Eric Latham to give me a release, and went back playing amateur. I wasn't good enough to play professionally anymore, or I wasn't dedicated enough I would say. I was in my thirties then, that's no age now but back then you weren't full-time, and you had no money. I had a job and was earning decent money, I didn't feel I needed to play professionally anymore, so I got it out of my system by playing amateur rugby. I loved it, I played until I was 41.

KEVIN IRO

Kevin Iro

CENTRE 1999–2001
HERITAGE NUMBER 1090

BORN: 25 May 1968, Auckland, New Zealand

SIGNED: 1999 from Auckland Warriors

DEBUT: 27 February 1999 vs Leeds Rhinos

LAST GAME: 6 October 2001 vs Wigan Warriors

ST HELENS CAREER: 84 appearances (including 1 as a substitute), 42 tries

HONOURS: Super League 1999, 2000; Challenge Cup 2001; World Club Challenge 2001

LEFT: 2001 retired

PLAYING CAREER: Wigan (1987–91), Manly (1991–92), Leeds (1992–96), Hunter Mariners (1997), Auckland Warriors (1998), St Helens (1999–2001)

Kevin Iro was already a household name by the time he arrived at Knowsley Road in 1999. 'The Beast' had broken the hearts of many Saints supporters over the years – especially at Wembley in 1989 – and it was now their turn to watch him at his flowing best in the Red Vee.

Iro was a strong-running centre with pace to burn. His spells at Wigan and Leeds – with a season at Manly in between

– saw him becoming a big name in English rugby league. He left England again in 1997 and had spells in the NRL with Hunter Mariners and Auckland Warriors.

It was a little bit of a surprise when Iro was announced as a St Helens player for the start of the 1999 season; he was in his thirties and a lot of people thought he was just coming over for a last payday.

That could not be further from the truth. During his three seasons at the Saints, Iro won the Super League Grand Final twice, the Challenge Cup Final and the World Club Challenge once. This was no holiday for 'The Beast'.

Despite his obvious links to fierce rivals Wigan, the Saints supporters took to Iro like one of their own and seemed to forget all the times he had been on the winning side AGAINST the Saints. Iro is a massive part of the club's history and his name will go down alongside some of the greatest to ever play for the club.

St Helens 16-11 Bradford Bulls

Super League Qualifying Play-Off
Friday, 22 September 2000
Knowsley Road, St Helens
Attendance 8,864

Teams

St Helens	*Bradford Bulls*
Paul Wellens	Stuart Spruce
Sean Hoppe	Tevita Vaikona
Kevin Iro	Michael Withers
Paul Newlove	Scott Naylor
Anthony Sullivan	Leon Pryce
Tommy Martyn	Henry Paul
Sean Long	Paul Deacon
Apollo Perelini	Paul Anderson
Keiron Cunningham	James Lowes
Julian O'Neill	Brian McDermott
Chris Joynt	Jamie Peacock
Tim Jonkers	Mike Forshaw
Paul Sculthorpe	Brad Mackay

Subs

Steve Hall	Robbie Paul
Dwayne West	Nathan McAvoy
John Stankevitch	Hudson Smith
Fereti Tuilagi	Stuart Fielden

Coaches

Ian Millward	Matthew Elliott

Tries

Hoppe	Peacock
Martyn	Pryce
Joynt	

Goals

Long (2)	Henry Paul

Drop Goal

	Henry Paul

Referee: Russell Smith

OK, it will be easier to start off this chapter with a little bit of commentary to get you in the mood – try and read this in your best Eddie and Stevo impression.

Hemmings: 'It's going be the match for Bradford.'

Stephenson: 'He's given a penalty.'

Hemmings: 'Oh, he has.'

Stephenson: 'He'd called held there. They're still not out of it. Oh, they've taken a short one, they know they've only got ten seconds. Will they get this play-the-ball in? They're holding him down.'

Crowd [counting down until the end of the match]:

'5, 4, 3, 2, 1'

Hemmings: 'Sculthorpe wants to get on with it, Bradford: counting down.'

Stephenson: 'Kick and chase now?'

Hemmings: 'This is the last play. Long … kicks it wide to Iro. Iro to Hall. Hall is trapped. Back it goes to Hoppe. Over the shoulder to Hall. There is Jonkers. Here is Long, and Long fancies it. Long fancies it. It's wide to West. It's wide to West. Dwayne West. Inside to Joynt. Joynt. JOYNT. JOYNT! OH! OH! FANTASTIC!'

Stephenson: 'I wouldn't believe it!'

Hemmings: 'They've won it, they've won it, they've won it. Chris Joynt; Chris Joynt has won it. It is unbelievable here, it is, frankly, unbelievable. Chris Joynt has won the match for St Helens.'

I'm out of breath just reading that now, never mind doing it live in front of millions of people. You have to admit, that is probably one of the best pieces of sports commentary that you will ever witness – and the rugby on show wasn't bad either.

I don't think it's a crime to admit to not knowing a great deal about what went on in that game until that moment. It was a great game, but the ending puts everything else in the shade. It was pure drama, and St Helens were probably the only team in that league that could have produced such a great team try with no time left on the clock.

During this chapter, Kevin Iro remembers what it was like to be on the field at that time and why he believed whoever won that game would go on to be champions. He also admits that he was quite naïve when it came to understanding the Wigan v St Helens rivalry when he was younger, but he understands it now.

I think this is a great game to choose because us and Bradford were like arch enemies at that particular time. Actually, we were rivals for the few seasons I was at St Helens and that game was a big one in terms of the play-offs – the winner was advancing and moving a step closer to the Grand Final.

It was at home at Knowsley Road, I had the feeling before the game that whoever won this match would actually go on and win the Grand Final. It was one of those games that we pulled it out of the fire right at the end, I still see it gets a lot of views. When I do watch that clip it really does bring back some good memories.

I was involved in the try that won the game. Longy [Sean Long] kicked the ball across the field. That was something that was good about that Saints team, a lot of teams would have panicked in that situation and tried to run it and put through a chip or a high kick, but Longy had the vision to kick across to see if we could break them down that side. We didn't, so we went back, and everyone just got behind the ball instead of panicking.

The hooter had gone, it was all over, I think the hooter went at the last play-the-ball. Longy had a stab and it didn't happen, so we went back, and of course young Dwayne West was there. Again, I think because he was young and green, he just had no fear either about panicking or putting a chip and chase through or something, he just beat the man, beat another and then turned the ball inside for Joynty [Chris Joynt] and he went over.

It was a good feeling. I think we played Wigan in the final, but we went to their place after this win over Bradford in the qualifying game and beat them convincingly to reach the Grand Final. I honestly just had that feeling that whoever won that game between us and Bradford would go on and be crowned champions. I think we were the two dominant sides of that time, and we always had real good battles with Bradford while I was at the club. It was always good to beat those guys because they were a hard team to beat, they were a big physical side back then.

How did my move to St Helens come about? I had played with Ellery [Hanley] obviously at Wigan and in Leeds, so when he took over the coaching job, he gave me a call to see if I would come over and play for Saints. When I look back at my time in St Helens, there were plenty of good times. That was probably the other memorable game during my first year at Saints, when we won the Grand Final against Bradford at Old Trafford. So, Ellery got me over and we managed to pull off the Grand Final win, so that was quite memorable for me. I think Ellery was only at St Helens for one season, and then Ian Millward took over and we had quite a bit of success under Ian as well.

I was very fortunate to be in some good English teams, I started off with Wigan and had a lot of success, and then to finish off at Saints and have just as much success was a really good run for me. I was very lucky.

Did I understand the rivalry between Saints and Wigan? I think because I was not a local lad – I was an overseas player – when we were at Wigan, we sort of knew who the derby games would be against, but I didn't really have an idea at all, plus I was much older when I got to Saints and then I realised how big the games were. When I was at Wigan, I didn't have a clue on how big they were, I was just young and didn't really think about those things. Obviously, the Wigan boys when they were playing Saints, they got more hyped up, and also when I was at Wigan it was the same thing when they played the Wire as well, they got hyped up about that game. By the time I got to Saints, I started realising, 'Hang on, there is something in these sort of local derby games,' particularly the Saints v Wigan ones.

I kind of knew when I signed for Saints that this would be my final club. I think I was around 30 when I signed for Saints and I thought I had a few years left in me. When I joined the club, I did have thoughts about whether it would be my last year, but I ended up having a hernia operation at the end of that 1999 season and I came right. I had a couple of years left in me after that operation. I honestly think if I didn't have that hernia operation, I probably would have quit that year. It kind of sorted me out. I had carried that problem for a few years and I just thought I was getting older and slower, but as soon as I had the hernia operation, I sort of had another surge in me.

It was my wife's decision for me to finish playing really, because we had four kids at that time, and we were away from family. She was basically bringing them up by herself because we were still living in Leeds, so I was in Lancashire most of the time travelling and training every day. She said to me, 'I've made the decision,' and that was it. We came straight back to Island (Arorangi) and we have been here ever since. I'm not involved in the game that much nowadays. I help out with some of the local teams in both union and league. They are shortened seasons over here, there are 12 games of league and 12 of union so kids can play both. I'm not involved in the NRL; the brother [Tony] has been involved with the NRL for years now, I think he's been with the Warriors for over ten years.

I follow the games in England when I can, we don't get any television coverage of the UK games, just a little bit of online stuff that I follow. We get the NRL here so I'm still watching the NRL coverage, but not the UK stuff. But I do really enjoy the UK stuff when I get to watch it, obviously there are a lot of boys that I used to play against or play with that are coaching there now. So, it's nice to see how they are doing.

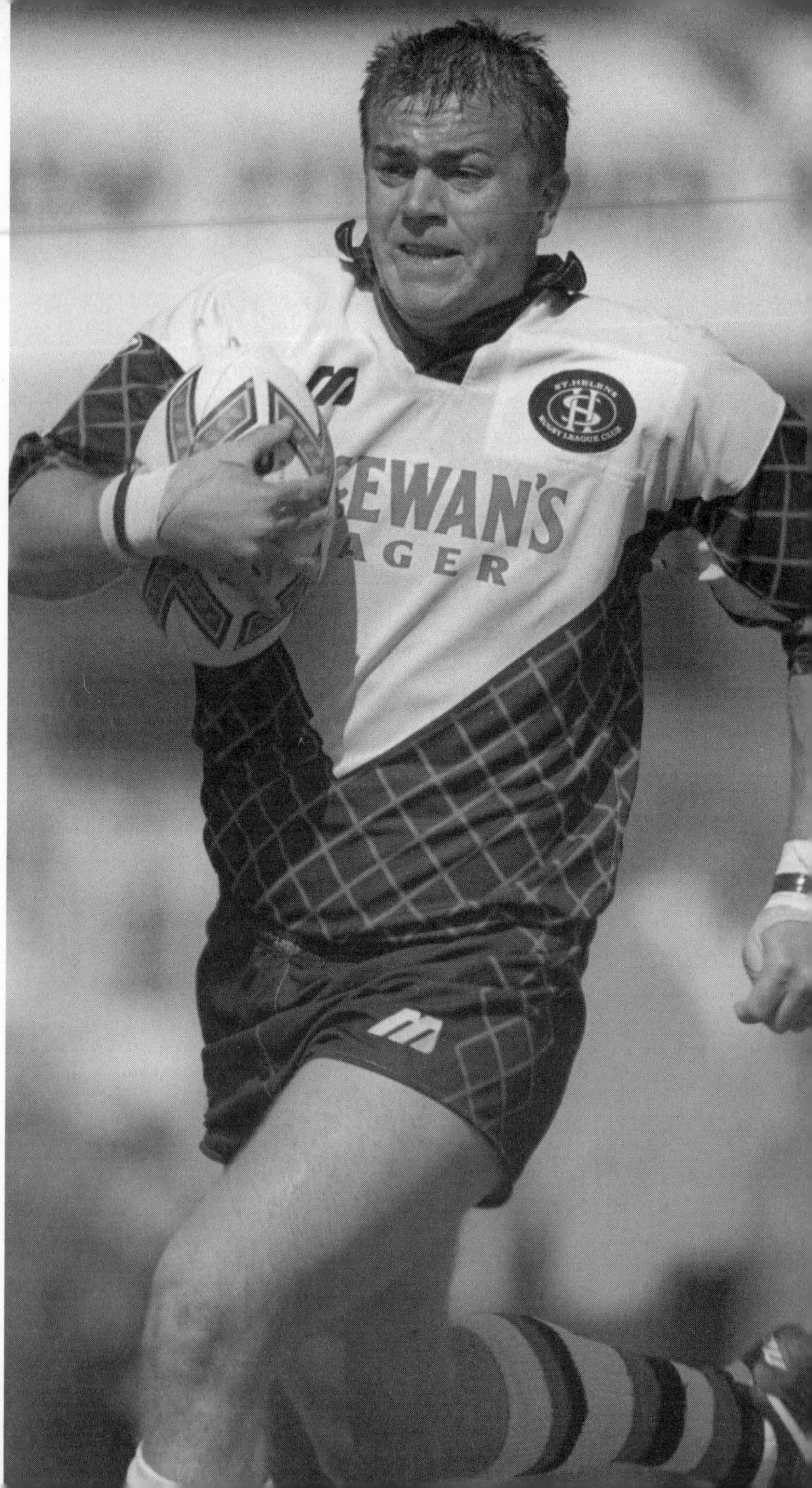

KARLE HAMMOND

Karle Hammond

STAND-OFF 1995–98
HERITAGE NUMBER 1061

BORN: 25 April 1974, Widnes, England

SIGNED: 7 July 1995 from Widnes

DEBUT: 13 September 1995 vs Sheffield Eagles

LAST GAME: 18 October 1998 vs Leeds Rhinos

ST HELENS CAREER: 111 appearances (including 9 as a substitute), 50 tries, 5 drop goals

HONOURS: Challenge Cup 1996, 1997; Super League 1996;

LEFT: 1998 to join London Broncos

PLAYING CAREER: Widnes (1993–95), St Helens (1995–98), London Broncos (1999–2000), Widnes (2001), Salford Red Devils (2001), Halifax (2002)

It is difficult to find many people who ever had a problem with Karle Hammond. Even fans from other clubs have commented that Hammond was a class player who probably should have won more trophies.

Hammond was a true professional and was born into the game thanks to his dad. He started his career at his home-town club Widnes and after a brief spell in Australia, he came back to England and joined St Helens ahead of the Centenary season.

During his time with the Saints, he managed to score 50 tries and left the club a Super League winner and a two-time Challenge Cup winner. During this chapter, he admits he wished he had stayed at Saints and fought for his place. It is his one main regret from his playing career.

The Hammond name holds some weight in the world of rugby league, and Karle will be hoping another member of the family will soon be making his name in the game. His teenage son has already admitted he wants to do a gap year and spend 12 months training with St Helens – watch this space.

St Helens 40-32 Bradford Bulls
Challenge Cup Final
Saturday, 27 April 1996
Wembley Stadium, London
Attendance 78,550

Teams
St Helens	*Bradford Bulls*
Steve Prescott	Nathan Graham
Danny Arnold	Paul Cook
Scott Gibbs	Matt Calland
Paul Newlove	Paul Loughlin
Anthony Sullivan	Jon Scales
Karle Hammond	Graeme Bradley
Bobbie Goulding	Robbie Paul
Apollo Perelini	Brian McDermott
Keiron Cunningham	Bernard Dwyer
Andy Leathem	Jon Hamer
Chris Joynt	Jeremy Donougher
Simon Booth	Sonny Nickle
Andy Northey	Simon Knox

Subs
Tommy Martyn | Karl Fairbank
Ian Pickavance | Paul Medley
Vila Matautia | Jason Donohue
Alan Hunte | Carlos Hassan

Coaches
Shaun McRae | Brian Smith

Tries
Arnold (2) | Paul (3)
Prescott (2) | Dwyer
Booth | Scales
Cunningham |
Perelini |
Pickavance |

Goals
Goulding (4) | Cook (6)

Referee: Stuart Cummings

Karle Hammond was a huge part of the St Helens team that won the double in 1996, so it is no surprise that he has chosen the 1996 Challenge Cup Final win over Bradford Bulls as his favourite game.

The win at Wembley was massive for the club; this was the first time St Helens had won the Challenge Cup since they beat Widnes in 1976, and every member of that cup-winning side will have a special place in the heart of every St Helens RLFC supporter.

Hammond uses this chapter to explain how the build-up went leading up to that game at Wembley, and also how coach Shaun McRae gave every single player a massive spray in the changing room during the half-time break for not sticking to their jobs.

That spray worked and Hammond goes on to fondly remember Bobbie Goulding bombing Nathan Graham to death with his high balls. Hammond also recalls dancing his way through the Bradford defence on the way to the try line, but his legs wouldn't carry him all the way and he had to give the ball to Danny Arnold to avoid a very embarrassing moment.

He also fondly remembers acting the clown with the late Steve Prescott to ensure they got on the pages of every national newspaper.

Hammond also opens up about his life in Australia and how he has managed to work through three different trades since moving away, with none of them being the one on his application form to get into the country.

I was a 1974 baby, born in Widnes. My dad was an ex-player with Widnes. So, I basically grew up on rugby league and following dad about. Dad used to take me to all the games, I was always around the club and the players and that was a successful era for going to Wembley and cup finals. There was the one in 1981 against Hull KR, I think, I don't remember much of that, but that was the first one I went to, then again there was the 1982 final with Hull and then your 1984 final with Wigan, and yeah my football as they call it over in Australia, my rugby took precedence over school and everything.

It was just in the blood, type of thing. Wembley was amazing; you have heard many a player over the years say that Wembley was the Mecca. I am far away from the game now, but it just seems that from what I watch, it [the cup final] has lost a bit of its magic with the Super League era and the attendances. It was always a big day out back in the day, for all rugby towns with it being towards the back end of the season.

Going on to my career, I had just come to the end of my time with Widnes and I had a bit of a stint over in Australia with the Roosters in 1995, then Saints came knocking and it was just one of them things where you knew it was bubbling nicely. A few of my mates were there, obviously Bobbie (Goulding) was keen to get me there. Like I say, it was just bubbling, they were the nearly-men but there was something happening underneath the surface.

I signed for Saints in that Centenary season, that was a massive step in my career. I was like a small cog going to a really big machine type of thing. Just from that, we knew we were building as a team and we were always building towards the 1996 Super League season. It was the era of being full-time. For me, as a kid I had plenty of common sense, but when it came to school, I was thick as pig shit, so to be working full-time in rugby league at Saints was brilliant.

We then signed Newy [Paul Newlove] just after me and everything started to work out. The club then brought in Bomber McRae [Shaun McRae] on the coaching side of it. It was always in the back of your mind, well for me anyway, that Wembley was coming up and I actually can't even remember the draw we got. I know we played Widnes, which was the club I had just left, in the semi-final. That was the start of the Wembley build-up; when you play in a semi-final there is a feeling that you can't get at any other time, knowing that you are going to Wembley.

It's a massive achievement and we were all on a high by just winning the semi-final against Widnes; it was just rammed straight down our throats that it's not a day out, we had only got to the final. Bomber McRae was really good with the man management side of it. The problem you had back then and we used to notice it a lot, was that you would have a lot of games between the semi-final and the final, and it was just emphasised that you cannot go into Wembley soft, you had to go in with the mentality of that winning feeling, which Wigan obviously had for almost a decade with winning at Wembley. You had to win going into the final, and that was the goal we set straight after winning the semi-final.

I remember the week before Wembley, we had played Halifax and everybody was off their game, and it was obvious why. Shaun just emphasised that there were places up for grabs now. So, we got through the Wembley week, it was just on my mind all the time that week. Even the day before, you know, actually I think it was two days before, you get to your hotel, and then the day before the game we went out to Eton College and had a training session there.

It was massive, I am pretty sure one of the royal family's princes was at Eton College at that time. It was just an amazing build-up, it was perfect.

We got to Wembley, we had a few experienced players that were getting everyone to relax and not play the game before. Obviously, Bobbie was really good with the team and that was one of the main things, we were not getting carried away and using up all our energy beforehand. We went around the stadium the day before. The ground is so influential when you realise what has happened there in the past. All the TV replays you have seen of the 1966 World Cup Final, the concerts and all the soccer finals, being a Liverpool supporter as well, Wembley was just a special place.

To go around the stadium before the game, basically like a private venue – though you couldn't train on it, because they always wanted the pitch to be in perfect condition – but we did the walk around and you just remember some of the things and the experience of it, you try to enjoy it without using up your energy. We were given talks about how much adrenaline you would get on the day of a game. Then as you travel to Wembley you have got everyone waving at you from outside and it's just a white noise of spectators and sirens going off. Then we had a police escort into the tunnel, it's just everything about the day, I just cannot think of a better experience. It is almost like you have played your career by that game, there was so much happening on that day before we had even kicked a ball or run the ball in anger.

I remember walking out, that was another thing where we were just walking out, and it was emphasised that once you go out of the tunnel you've got around 20 or 30 minutes of waiting around. We were stood in the tunnel and I was looking across, Bradford were playing the game already; they were shouting out different plays that we had that they knew what they were called. I remember thinking, 'jeez calm down boys, we've not even kicked off yet'. I could see how anxious they were. I can't even remember the score of the first half, but I always felt we were in control and still going to win the game.

We went in at the break and I think Preccy [Steve Prescott] had scored a couple of tries, I'm not sure if he had got one or two by then, then Robbie Paul had done a bit of his magic. We just knew we were in control and went in at half-time and just got a massive spray off Shaun McRae because we were just giving Bradford too much respect, we weren't putting the back three, as in the two wingers and full-back, under any pressure and they were playing well.

He gave us this spray about not putting any pressure on and we went out for the second half, I think Robbie Paul had scored the second of his tries and I can't remember whether there was a try again – actually yeah, Bernard [Dwyer] scored for them. This is another thing that always comes to mind, it was Bernard that scored but I remember looking at the clock and something like 56 minutes had gone, I might be mistaken but I remember thinking, pardon my French, 'Fuck, this is not a good place to lose'. That was the very first time during the game that I thought, 'shit we are going to have to do something friggin' special here because we are going to lose and everything we have worked for is going to be up the swanny.'

We were behind the posts and it was 26-12 or something like that, we were saying 'we need to score next'. It's only now when I think about Bomber McRae giving us that spray about not putting enough pressure on the back three and then I think about Bobbie's kicks. More so our chase, we put them under so much pressure and poor Nathan Graham got a bit of the blame, but he got no help at all and I've seen a few clips – I've never watched the full game back but I have seen the clips – and I thought 'bloody hell, the back players didn't give him any help'. We had amazing kicks and amazing chases and we competed for everything and it just fell into someone's hands. As soon as we took the lead it was like, 'We are going to rattle up a few more points'. Keiron [Cunningham] made a break up the middle like he always did, he threw off about three players and got the ball out to Gibbsy [Scott Gibbs] and Gibbsy got it to me. I managed to step someone and threw a couple of dummies and the bloody try line was right in front of me and I was just absolutely gassed, there was nothing in my legs and I was just trying to get to this line. It was like I was running in quicksand and then one of the back rowers just got me about two metres from the line but with enough time for me to pass to Danny [Arnold] on my right. He was screaming for a good ten seconds while I was throwing dummies all over the place and trying to get over the line to try and get a little meat pie. I got him the ball and we were well ahead by then and I just always remember it was in the right-hand corner towards the tunnel and I just stayed on both my knees. I was looking up to the sky and just fist pumping and thinking, 'It doesn't get any better than this, this is just everything I ever wanted coming true.'

You could almost feel the heat touching you in that stadium and the noise was phenomenal. You can't explain it, I never really tried to compare that to anything. I played at Wembley two times after that in 1997 and 1999 and it was nothing compared to that one in 1996. We tried to take things into the games, but I got flogged with London in 1999. We were in the game for a while, but players were just watching the clock while we were in the game and you can't do that at Wembley.

You have got to conserve all your energy, especially in that 1996 match. Time seemed to stand still, until we were trailing 26-12 and from that minute until the 80th it was just like a video game where you are just clawing your way back and keep putting the pressure on. That final siren goes, and it is total euphoria that takes over. There was a lot of talk about the bridesmaid thing with Saints because it was back in the seventies when they last won the Challenge Cup. We just kept hearing about the bridesmaid tag and losing at Wembley with the Halifax loss and the two against Wigan in 1989 and 1991. It wasn't just that it took the monkey off the back, but we showed what it takes to be a successful team. There were plenty of games at the back end of 1996 when they were all games that we thought we were going to lose. I remember Apollo [Perelini] scoring late on against London Broncos, but we were always ready to compete. That Warrington game at the end, that was just 80 minutes that seemed like a couple of minutes.

But when we won at Wembley, that is what you remember. You remember that trophy, it's an amazing cup. We were all gathered together talking and the stewards were getting us over into one spot. It was funny because there was always me and Preccy that were doing something stupid or messing about and I said to Preccy, 'Let's get behind Bobbie here and we'll get in all the newspaper photographs and all the TV programmes.' When you see it, it's Bobbie then me and Preccy going berserk, we always had a giggle about that. Then the next year, I tried to make sure I was last up there so I could get the cup. I can't actually remember where I was on that one, but for 1996 I was only 22 at the time, but I still say now that I could have easily retired right then. It was absolutely amazing. I had three years and four seasons at Saints and I still look back at that time, I still have dreams and I wake up thinking, 'Why the fuck did I leave Saints?'

I knew something had to happen because there were times when they were trying to get Iestyn Harris from Warrington and then we got Scully [Paul Sculthorpe] so it was only a matter of time before Scully was going to get his rightful spot in the Saints Hall of Fame. You think now, I could have just filled in around the back row or filled in the halves when Tommy [Martyn] was out, but I never got that feeling I was wanted. If I had got a call off Ellery [Hanley] saying 'we would like you to stay' it might have been different, but I was getting to the stage – I would have been about 24 or 25 – where I thought I would be behind Tommy and Scully and I wanted to have more say and more chance to do things, so I started talking to a couple of clubs and I just liked the idea of the London setup and that's the only reason I left Saints, because I was totally away from the north and not thinking about it.

I was still in two minds but the offer was good from London and it was away from what I was used to and I wouldn't be thinking 'what the bloody hell have I done' type of thing. I always think I should have just stayed at Saints, but I wanted to be the main ball player, and that was the only way I was going to get it at a club that was trying to get up at the top. I suppose in a way London did, we got to the final in my first year. It was a strange setup at the Broncos because by the time I had signed for them around the time of the 1998 Grand Final, they had already got rid of the coach that had signed me in Tony Currie. Then by the end of 1999 they had got rid of that coach and they were going to move from west London to the south. I just got side-tracked. I didn't like the new coach, I didn't get on with John Monie anyway.

Once I messaged you and said that 1996 was the game I would choose, I started to think there was about 20 games that stand out. It's not always the actual game that is memorable, it's the players. I formed a great bond with Huntey [Alan Hunte] on the right-hand side, I started to struggle once Huntey left to be honest. He was such a clever player and he took so much pressure off the left side because all the defences were concentrating on Tommy and Newy and Sully (Anthony Sullivan) on that side and me and Huntey would just have a field day because all the lazy defenders would be hiding on the left-hand side. You couldn't believe it in a professional code, you even see it now that the dominant side is passing from right to left; if you are playing football you need to be able to pass as well left to right, but to get a centre like Huntey who would run all day, like I say, we had a ball on that side. Huntey would just be naming players to look for and we just had a combo. Then he left in 1998 and we just started to get a little bit stale. I think it showed in some performances that year, I think we still got to the main semi-final for the first Grand Final, I think it was Leeds that knocked us out, so we still had the talent but we didn't have the mental attitude that we had the last two years.

That's football, I'm just disappointed that Wembley is not the main attraction now. Back in the day, when it was at the end of April and beginning of May, you would have people going for weekends because it was at the end of the season. In an ideal world, you would play less games now and be able to finish the Grand Final in September, when it is normally still hot down south and you would get that atmosphere again, but it's just like another stadium now, whereas then Wembley meant something and had a lot of history connected with it, the Twin Towers and all that. When we used to go as supporters, you would get off the train and you suddenly got around the corner and you would just see the big Twin Towers and Wembley Way, it was just awesome. It's easy to say awesome because you can't think of a better word to describe those trips to Wembley.

I'm still a Saints fan at heart, hopefully one of my boys will follow in my footsteps and head back over, one of them actually wants to. How did I move to Australia? I have always liked the lifestyle and the weather, just the environment for the kids with all the sport there. They always loved rugby, but they were at an age where they hadn't started playing in the UK. We had about six years just outside of Sydney towards Wollongong, I thought it was apt then because I could go for the Saints in Australia and the Saints in the UK type of thing. I was even more pleased when Jammer [James Graham] came and signed for the Dragons. I'm just happy the kids are back rugby training now after all this Covid-19 stuff.

My lads are keen to go back to the UK to see Nanna and Grandad and the 17-year-old now is at that stage where he is playing a lot of rugby and he keeps saying he wants to go and do an off-season with Saints and live with Nanna and Grandad. He probably will, he's looking at being with a feeder club for the North Queensland

Cowboys and then transferring from that feeder club to one in Brisbane when he goes to university to study to become a PE teacher. He is then looking at taking a gap year and training then, so we'll see what happens. It's a great setup over here for the kids. In the UK I always found there were two separate things with BARLA and the junior football, but here everything is connected. Your membership with your junior club gets you into your local NRL games, even though the Cowboys in Townsville is like four hours away from us in Cairns, we are in the far north of Queensland. It is all connected, they have training modules and they are all similar at each club, plus the weather helps. They have coaching days and training days to help them learn off and to be close to the big clubs. There are a lot of talented kids and there is no reason why they can't make it, but there is just a mountain of kids vying for one position here.

I have done a few things while I have been out here. I did about five years in New South Wales working in the mines. I got into the mine work, the pay was good and even when I moved to Queensland, I was set to work in the mines again, but I ended up working in the prison up here. So, I had six years as a prison guard, which is a bit different up here in the far north. It was a strange old job. I have done work in the funeral business as well, I have done a diploma in mortuary science, basically when you get that qualification you can work around Australia then in different hospitals and funeral parlours. That is probably the most satisfying job that I have had outside of rugby. I help with the families and that type of thing so yeah, I have had three totally different trades while I've been here.

I got accepted into the country as a plumber because that's what job I had before being a full-time player. I came out as a plumber and never touched a tool while being out here. I started in the mines because the club I was coaching with in New South Wales had a contract with them, so they fixed us up with that job and then I moved up to Atherton near Cairns and that was the club that took Todd Carney on when he was a bit wayward, so I did some coaching there and that's when I moved into the prison. Then I went back to school and did my diploma. It's all good. It's not all unicorns and rainbows, you have to work hard to put food on the table. I think that is the main thing in life: to have food on the table and healthy kids.

One Final Point

I thought long and hard about putting this next part of the Karle Hammond interview into the book. As I have already mentioned, I have been suffering with mental health issues such as depression and anxiety. Karle knew about this and he offered these words as we finished the interview. I think by printing this, it helps send the message that anyone can be affected by mental health issues, but more importantly there is always someone out there who is willing to listen.

Karle Hammond: 'Look after yourself as well lad. I have had mental health issues in the past with depression and things like that.'

David Kuzio: 'Thanks. I finally just admitted it after a few years, I just hit rock bottom and I needed to get it out.'

KH: 'I had so much anger. Even people at work, I was loving the confrontation type of thing with the prisoners and someone said, "You are going to end up dead, or more to the point, you are going to get one of us killed, Karle." It was mad, it was just like a depression where you felt down and sorry for yourself. Like you say, people that don't deal with it, think you can just snap out of it or take medication. But it takes a shitload of medication to find the right one that works with you.'

DK: 'Yeah, I found that. I was on some tablets that didn't do anything and then they doubled the strength and I was just falling asleep all the time. Then they had to halve that again, but I am getting there. A month ago, this book was nowhere near finished and I could be finishing it this week.'

KH: 'It's just your own personal trial and personal battle because only you can understand it. It's a bit like that in the funeral game, no one can tell someone who has just lost a parent or a brother or sister that you do this or that. You don't. There are no books for mental health or grief or happiness. One day you are going to be happy, then the next day it is like you are stood on a shitload of tacks. It takes a while to learn and tell your body that you are having a down day, take time out and think about it. It does take a while, if people are depending on you and you know they are depending on you, just think of them.'

DK: 'That's what I am trying to do. It's just getting through it and realising what you are here for.'

KH: 'It is, you are right. If all else fails, just have a look at Wigan getting beat or something.'

DK: 'Thanks for this mate.'

KH: 'No worries pal, take care.'

Janette Smith

Also available at all good book stores

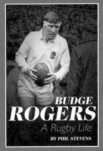

9781785311338

9781785315619

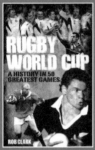

9781785310539

9781785310386

9781905411641

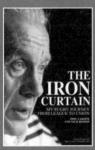

9781785310393